"Get wisdom!" So the father exhort[...] Proverbs (Prov 4:5). But what is wisdom and how do we become wise? In *Walking in God's Wisdom*, Benjamin Quinn deftly and winsomely guides us in the proper way to read the book of Proverbs in order to answer these important questions. I enthusiastically recommend this accessible yet profound book to all who want to grow in godly wisdom.

TREMPER LONGMAN III
Distinguished Scholar and Professor Emeritus
of Biblical Studies, Westmont College

A culture marked by the celebration and affirmation of folly particularly needs a helpful guide to biblical wisdom. This new book by Benjamin Quinn provides just that as he skillfully introduces the reader to the book of Proverbs. The book is accessible, engaging, and insightful. It will be a great benefit to study groups and individuals. I heartily commend it to you.

RAY VAN NESTE
dean, School of Theology and Missions;
professor of biblical studies, Union University

For those interested in pursuing godly wisdom, be sure to read Benjamin Quinn's *Walking in God's Wisdom* with a highlighter and a pen. In a clear and understandable way, he explains how the Bible's most practical book points to Jesus. This excellent resource would be a great fit for church small groups or Bible studies—or anyone looking to live like Jesus in an often foolish world.

SARAH ZYLSTRA
senior writer, The Gospel Coalition

The book of Proverbs enjoys a nostalgic warmth among its readers, which explains its place in many daily devotions. In truth, many of the sayings are difficult—some even shocking or impossible to understand. More than that, the full book of thirty-one chapters is rarely appreciated for its theological vision, poetic style, and clever wordplay. In his new book, Benjamin Quinn gives us two things in one. The first is his transformation of scholarly research on the most difficult questions into a winsome introduction for readers of every level. Second, Quinn helps us draw pleasure from the individual sayings while simultaneously gaining a vision for their place in the book and the theology of Scripture beyond.

RYAN O'DOWD
pastor, Bread of Life Anglican Church, Ithaca, New York; author of *Proverbs* (Story of God Bible Commentary)

Walking in God's Wisdom is primarily about correcting our spiritual vision rather than developing in us spiritual dexterity and balance. Through this insightful, concise reading of Proverbs, Benjamin Quinn prescribes the right lenses to see God's world according to who God is and how he designed it. In laying out this view, Quinn offers what he aptly terms a "guiding perspective" by which we are called to walk skillfully in the light of Christ, who is both the very wisdom of God and the light of the world. In the knowledge of Christ and his glorious light, we learn the life-giving way of Godfearers, who (wisely) resist folly and love righteousness.

KEITH S. WHITFIELD
provost, Southeastern Baptist Theological Seminary

WALKING IN GOD'S WISDOM

THE BOOK OF PROVERBS

Other titles in the Transformative Word series

Visit lexhampress.com/transformative-word

WALKING IN GOD'S WISDOM

THE BOOK OF PROVERBS

TRANSFORMATIVE WORD

BENJAMIN T. QUINN

Series Editors
Craig G. Bartholomew &
David J. H. Beldman

LEXHAM PRESS

Walking in God's Wisdom: The Book of Proverbs
Transformative Word

Lexham Press, 1313 Commercial St., Bellingham, WA 98225
LexhamPress.com

Print ISBN 9781683594796
Digital ISBN 9781683594802
Library of Congress Control Number 2021933207

Series Editors: Craig G. Bartholomew and David J. H. Beldman
Lexham Editorial: David Bomar, Allisyn Ma, Mandi Newell, and
    Abigail Salinger
Cover Design: Joshua Hunt
Typesetting: Fanny Palacios

To Mom and Dad

(Proverbs 1:8–9)

TABLE OF CONTENTS

ACKNOWLEDGMENTS

To the LifeChange Class at North Wake Church—thank you for your interest and feedback in my teaching of Proverbs. Your insights and questions were invaluable in helping me better understand and articulate the wisdom of Proverbs. Special thanks to Dr. Jerry Lassetter and Dr. Chip McDaniel, who taught with me in this class and were ever-wise conversation partners as we worked through the material.

To Holly Grove Baptist Church—you showed such grace and patience as I taught this material in the early months of serving as your pastor. Thank you for your love and support!

To Kay Smith—thank you for your hours of proofreading and advice on the manuscript.

To Craig Bartholomew and David Beldman—for the invitation to contribute to this series, and for your patience and wise counsel throughout.

To Lexham Press—for your willingness to publish and your sage advice in fine-tuning the final form of the manuscript.

To Ashley—the greatest model of the Proverbs 31 woman I've ever seen (Prov 31:28).

INTRODUCTION
TO PROVERBS

Get wisdom; get insight: do not forget, nor turn away
from the words of my mouth. Do not forsake her, and
she will keep you; love her, and she will guard you.
The beginning of wisdom is this: Get wisdom, and
whatever else you get, get insight.

—Proverbs 4:5-7

"Get Wisdom!"—Personal Interest in Proverbs

I recall the first time I read Proverbs 4:5-7. The words
leaped off the page with urgency and passion. In fact, one
translation renders the beginning of verse 7, "Wisdom is
supreme—so get wisdom" (HCSB). It's too bad the trans-
lators didn't include exclamation points to capture the
force of the three imperatives in this passage, which
builds in intensity from "love her!" to "get wisdom!" to
"get insight!"

Somewhere in my early teenage years, I was struck by the emphasis of verse 7: "Get wisdom!" It felt as though this was equally as strong as the New Testament imperatives I was familiar with, such as "love God and neighbor" or "go, therefore, and make disciples." Could it be that "get wisdom" carries as much punch as the Great Commandment and the Great Commission?

This set me on a journey to understand better what wisdom is, what it does, and how it works in God's world, specifically in the Christian life. Growing up, my dad frequently urged my brothers and me to be wise men and make wise decisions. On the one hand, I knew exactly what he meant. But on the other, I struggled to understand, much less articulate, what wisdom is and does. This eventually led to doctoral studies on how St. Augustine understood wisdom. I thought: Who better to learn from about wisdom than arguably the most influential theologian in history, who also—and I do not find this a coincidence—spoke more about wisdom than any other theologian in history? And now, several years removed from that study, I'm still gripped by it.

I've come to believe that "get wisdom!" in Proverbs 4:7 bears as much weight as better-known imperatives from Scripture. As such, this book offers an introduction to the book of Proverbs specifically through the lens of the central theme of wisdom, addressing what it is, what it does, how it relates to the whole book of Proverbs as well as the rest of the Bible, and why it matters for Christian living at all times and in all places. Rather ambitious, I know. But wisdom is no small thing.

Approach to Proverbs

Above all, Proverbs is God's worldwide invitation to "get wisdom!" This is accomplished not however we please, but specifically by beginning our journey in the fear of the Lord, then walking God's way in all of life. This parallels Jesus' parable in Matthew 7:24–27, where he teaches that the wise person is the one who "hears these words of mine and does them" (ESV). This is like a man who built his house on a rock that was able to withstand the storm. The foolish person, however, heard but didn't heed Jesus' instruction, like a man who built his house on sand that was destroyed by the storm. Proverbs issues the same call to hear and obey wisdom—to walk God's way.

This book offers a broad but brief introduction to how we can walk God's way according to Proverbs. We will focus the bulk of our attention on the themes found in the first nine chapters of Proverbs, followed by a look at Proverbs 31 and practical themes. This approach serves to frame our reading and experience of Proverbs in light of the whole Bible and in accord with the author's intent. Along the way, we'll examine Proverbs' overall coherence and unity, which is often missed in a proverb a day readings and devotionals.

> "Proverbs is the foundational wisdom book of the Bible, teaching the ABC's of wisdom."
>
> —Raymond C. Van Leeuwen, "Book of Proverbs" in *Dictionary of Theological Interpretion of the Bible*

The book of Proverbs eludes many common interpretive approaches as it is a unique genre in the Bible.[1] According to most scholars, Proverbs is primarily poetry that often uses personification to illustrate key themes (such as Lady Wisdom and Lady Folly in Prov 9). But it is more than mere poetry. It includes prose, direct instruction like that found in an epistle, as well as satire and irony. Further, for Proverbs, historical context and social setting are notoriously difficult to determine—and, strangely, they seem largely insignificant as the teaching of the book transcends specific times and places, being applicable to all times and places.[2] Yet, ironically, wise action is heavily dependent on discernment of specific times and places. Such is the nature of God's wisdom.

For other books of the Bible, recognizing the historical context is an imperative and a basic aspect of good interpretation—a first step, as it were, to proper Bible reading. Proverbs is distinct in this way, disrupting conventional Bible study methods. This in no way means that Proverbs is ahistorical, as though it has no context. Nor does it suggest that history is unimportant in Proverbs. Quite the opposite, in fact. I would argue that wisdom literature in general, and Proverbs in particular, promotes a high view of God's action in his world, and thus a high view of time, place, and history.[3]

Nevertheless, a unique book requires a unique, though responsible, approach—an approach that is sensitive to the book's content and literary type, and that considers the content in light of the broader context and teaching of Scripture. Such is our approach, as will be further discussed in the next chapter.

Date and Authorship

The date and authorship of Proverbs is difficult to determine, as the book is a collection of wisdom (wise sayings) from various places over a long period of time. King Solomon is first acknowledged as an author/collector of much of Proverbs (Prov 1:1; 10:1). Other sections of Proverbs are attributed to Hezekiah (25:1–29:27), Agur son of Jakeh (30:1–33), and King Lemuel (31:1–31).

Moreover, Proverbs was edited over several centuries, from as early as the time of Solomon (tenth century BC) possibly to as late as 330 BC, following Alexander the Great's conquest of Palestine.[4] Precise dating is uncertain, however, due to the lack of historical specificity in the book.[5] Most evangelical scholars view Proverbs as an earlier work, completed sometime between the tenth and fifth centuries BC. Additionally, Proverbs appears to incorporate wisdom from other traditions and cultures such as ancient Egypt and Mesopotamia, some of which predate Solomon.[6]

Outline of this Study

In this short introductory study, space will not allow for commentary on most chapters and verses in Proverbs. Instead, we will consider the nature of wisdom in Proverbs that will serve as the lens through which we will view other important themes.

Chapters 2 and 3 will consider first the contours of wisdom, followed by wisdom as the solution to the world's greatest problem. Here we will identify the core ingredients, as well as offer a brief discussion on the nature of a proverb and how Proverbs fits into the Bible as a whole.

This will illumine the problem/solution or folly/wisdom shape that many—though not all—proverbs take in Proverbs 10 and following, such as: "Evil plans are an abomination to the Lord [problem or folly], but gracious words are pure [solution or wisdom]" (Prov 15:26).

Chapters 4 through 6 will explore themes from Proverbs 1–9, giving particular attention to the dominant themes of way, knowledge, creation, Creator, and tradition, all through the primary lens of wisdom. Proverbs 1–9 lays the thematic groundwork for the rest of the book. Thus, this opening section functions like an introduction to the book while maintaining deep continuity with the overall purpose: "[to learn] about wisdom and instruction, for understanding words of insight, for gaining instruction in wise dealing, righteousness, justice, and equity; to teach shrewdness to the simple, knowledge and prudence to the young" (Prov 1:2–4).

Chapters 7 and 8 will consider the wise woman of Proverbs 31 and practical themes from the rest of Proverbs. In light of the framework and key themes discovered in the first six chapters of this book, we will recognize that the most ordinary aspects of life are packed with importance for wise living before God in his world.

STRUCTURE OF PROVERBS[7]

☐ 1:1–7, Preamble

☐ 1:8–9:18, Extended Discourses and Admonitions on Wisdom

☐ 10:1–22:16, First Collection of Solomon

☐ 22:17–24:34, Collected Sayings for a Son

☐ 25:1–29:27, Second Collection of Solomon

☐ 30:1–33, Agur and Wisdom in the Upside-Down World

☐ 31:1–9, Sayings of King Lemuel

☐ 31:10–31, Poem to the Wise Woman

SUGGESTED READING
☐ Proverbs 4:1–27

Reflection

How has Proverbs affected your life up to this point?

_____

_____

_____

Name three examples of wisdom from Proverbs that you have incorporated into your daily life (or are seeking to incorporate).

_____

_____

_____

What is one thing you wish to understand better about Proverbs? And what is one area of your life where you hope to apply the wisdom of Proverbs more faithfully?

_____

_____

_____

2

CONTOURS AND CORE INGREDIENTS OF WISDOM

Wisdom is the way of God made for humans to walk.

—Daniel J. Treier, *Proverbs & Ecclesiastes,*
Brazos Theological Commentary on the Bible

According to Scripture, wisdom is,
broadly speaking, knowledge of God's world and
the knack of fitting oneself into it.

—Cornelius Plantinga Jr. and Sue A. Rozeboom,
*Discerning the Spirits: A Guide to Thinking
about Christian Worship Today*

Contours of Wisdom

One of my favorite questions to ask people is, "How would you define wisdom?" It is an interesting question as I've never met anyone—Christian or not—who was uninterested in wisdom. In fact, many cultures and world religions have their own wisdom traditions promoting their view of a proper way of life.

The trouble with this question, though, is that wisdom is notoriously difficult to define. Wisdom is a "totality concept" as Raymond Van Leeuwen suggests (more on this in the next chapter), and defining it runs the risk of leaving something out or oversimplifying.[8] Nonetheless, we do want to be clear about our view of wisdom, so we'll begin by offering five essential ingredients of wisdom.[9] These, I trust, will light the way into our study of Proverbs and provide a unifying framework for the many themes and topics throughout the book.

Essential Ingredients of Wisdom

Ingredient #1: Wisdom Is an Attribute of God That Is Fully Revealed in Jesus

In this book, much of our attention will focus on the aspects of wisdom that are found in creation and that are gained over time through experience and instruction. To begin, though, we must recognize that wisdom is an attribute of God; and by wisdom he created the world (Prov 3 and 8). This divine quality is mysteriously etched into God's world, leaving traces of him in everything that has been made—both visible and invisible—and pointing all creation back to him "so that God may be all in all" (1 Cor 15:28). This is an important though delicate point; as we are not suggesting that in creating by wisdom God breached the important divide between Creator and creation. Instead, we must hold a more nuanced— even sophisticated—view of wisdom that allows us to understand it as both an attribute of God and a quality of God's creation that directs creatures toward proper living in his world.

Further, this divine wisdom is fully revealed in Jesus. We will address this further in chapter 5, but now we observe Paul's instruction that Jesus is "the power of God and the wisdom of God" (1 Cor 1:24), "in whom are hidden all the treasures of wisdom and knowledge" (Col 2:3).

Ingredient #2: Wisdom Is Grounded in the Fear of the Lord

The purpose statement for the book of Proverbs is given in the first seven verses of the book, especially verses 2–6. In summary, the purpose of Proverbs is

> for learning about wisdom and instruction,
>> for understanding words of insight,
> for gaining instruction in wise dealing,
>> righteousness, justice, and equity;
> to teach shrewdness to the simple,
>> knowledge and prudence to the young (1:2–4),

as well as to further instruct the wise in learning and skill (1:5).

Verse 7 is the keystone of the introduction, declaring that "the fear of the LORD is the beginning of knowledge; fools despise wisdom and instruction." The author will bookend this first major section of Proverbs (chapters 1–9) with a nuanced but similar declaration in 9:10: "The fear of the LORD is the beginning of wisdom, and knowledge of the Holy One is insight." We will give further attention to the meaning and importance of "the fear of the Lord" below, but suffice it to say at this point that without the fear of Yahweh—the God of Abraham, Isaac, Jacob, Moses, David, the prophets, Jesus, and the apostles—there is no true wisdom.

Ingredient #3: Wisdom Seeks to Live According to the Order That God Has Built into Creation

Proverbs 3:19-20 states, "The LORD by wisdom founded the earth; by understanding he established the heavens; by his knowledge the deeps broke open, and the clouds drop down the dew." It is tempting, perhaps, to read this passage and assume that it is simply a flashy description of God's exhaustive knowledge and ability to create. And, indeed, it is not less than that; but it is far more.

In this passage, Proverbs alerts us to the fact that God not only built his world by wisdom, but also built wisdom into his world. This shouldn't be confused with the "wisdom of the world" that Paul warns about (1 Cor 1:20; 3:19); instead this wisdom originates from God above (Jas 3:13-18) and is built into every nook and cranny of creation.

There is a pattern and order to God's world that promotes divine shalom, or flourishing, as God designed. In Genesis 3, however, sin entered the garden and wreaked havoc in God's world. Nevertheless, we must not think that what God made good, sin made bad. Instead, sin acts as a parasite on what God has made, seeking to pervert it, corrupt it, and direct it away from God. But it cannot negate its goodness, which belongs to the Lord.

As such, Proverbs often illustrates wisdom with created things that operate according to God's design.

THE ANT AS AN EXAMPLE OF GOD'S INTENDED DESIGN (PROV 6:6–11)

Proverbs 6:6–11 directs our attention to ants of all things to illustrate the virtue of hard work. Amid chastising the child who is lovingly referred to as "lazybones," the writer of Proverbs contrasts the lazy way of life with a wiser way of life exemplified by ants:

> Go to the ant, you lazybones;
>> consider its ways, and be wise.
>
> Without having any chief
>> or officer or ruler,
>
> it prepares its food in summer,
>> and gathers its sustenance in harvest.
>
> How long will you lie there, O lazybones?
>> When will you rise from your sleep?
>
> A little sleep, a little slumber,
>> a little folding of the hands to rest,
>
> and poverty will come upon you like a robber,
>> and want like an armed warrior.

Why ants? Is this an intentional moment of condescension by the wise teacher? Perhaps there is a hint of that, but more importantly, the teacher is highlighting the wisdom that God built into the world.

There is pattern and rhythm in creation that points creatures toward the way of the Creator. The way God built the world informs the way we ought to live. As quoted in the epigraph above by Daniel Treier, "Wisdom is the way of God made for humans to walk." Again, this shouldn't be confused with the ways of the world we are warned about. Instead, we recognize that the ways of the world run opposed to the way of the Lord. Those who fear the Lord are called to walk in his ways in his world, and how to do that is informed by what God has said and by what God has made.

Ingredient #4: Wisdom Focuses on Discerning God's Ways in Particular Circumstances

Often in my younger years, I was told that life is black and white—meaning, of course, that life is simple, and that proper decision-making is always clear and straightforward. However, I quickly encountered a problem with that philosophy: it doesn't work because it isn't true.

If life were black and white and easy to navigate, why would we need wisdom? Knowledge alone would suffice because discernment would be unnecessary. But this is not how life works. Our human experience often leaves us facing difficult decisions about money, marriage, friendships, work, parenting, discipline, etc.—all things that Proverbs addresses. Why? Because wisdom is required.

Decisions about these ordinary matters are not the same for every person. It may be wise for me to spend a lot of money on my youngest son for medical expenses because he's prone to ear infections, while it may not be wise for someone else's son who doesn't have the same condition. Instead, it may be wiser for him to spend a lot of money on gluten-free groceries due to his spouse's allergies.

In both cases, wisdom is applied, but the application of wisdom is different. It isn't one-size-fits-all; instead, wisdom is particularized to specific times and places. It considers the circumstances. Proverbs 26:4–5 illustrates this well:

> Do not answer fools according to their folly,
>   or you will be a fool yourself.
> Answer fools according to their folly,
>   or they will be wise in their own eyes.

Does Proverbs contradict itself here? Or might there be something in the nature of wisdom that suggests the wise response is not always the same? In one case, the fool may be teachable and willing to receive correction, so we answer him with correction. In another case, however, we may discern that the fool is *not* teachable. Thus, it would be foolish to waste our time offering correction. These two proverbs teach us that answering or not answering a fool requires wisdom.

This must not be understood as inconsistent, relativistic, or wisdom that is prone to favoritism. By no means! Instead, wisdom recognizes the uniqueness of specific times, places, and people and carefully applies love for God and neighbor to those circumstances.

Ingredient #5: Wisdom Is Rooted in Tradition

In the first chapter of Proverbs we read, "Hear, my child, your father's instruction, and do not reject your mother's teaching" (1:8). This parent-to-child, teacher-to-student voice that narrates much of Proverbs' early chapters signals the importance of wisdom that is handed down through generations. This tradition of wisdom is set in contrast to other wisdom traditions in the ancient world because it originates with Yahweh—the God of Abraham, Isaac, Jacob, Moses, and David (and eventually, Jesus and the apostles). And it begins with a fear of Yahweh. Other wisdom traditions are oriented toward other gods, but Proverbs is oriented toward the true God—the maker of heaven and earth.

This tradition dates to the beginning of time and space and remains through the end of time, even into eternity. This tradition leads the people of God in the ways of God, guiding us in the paths of righteousness for his name's sake. It includes the gospel of Jesus that is "the faith which was once for all delivered to the saints" (Jude 1:3 NKJV), a tradition Christians participate in and promote wherever Christ is proclaimed. It is also family-based. Derek Kidner rightly notes that while the family is not everything in Proverbs, "the home remains the place from which this teaching emanates, and whatever threatens its integrity is viewed here with profound concern."[10]

• • •

These five wisdom ingredients are not exhaustive. Yet they are central to the Bible's teaching about wisdom, especially in Proverbs, and serve to assist Godfearers everywhere as we journey through this great book about wise living in God's world.

SUGGESTED READING

☐ Proverbs 2:1–23

Reflection

Restate the essential ingredients of wisdom outlined above in your own words. How would you teach them to children and adults?

_____

_____

_____

Can you remember a time when the proper application of wisdom was determined by the situation (the fourth ingredient)? How did the particular time, place, and person(s) involved inform wise action?

_____

_____

_____

_____

3

WISDOM—THE CLUE TO WORLDVIEW

PROVERBS 1–9

> The wise person knows creation. She knows
> its boundaries and limits, understands its laws
> and dynamics, discerns its times and seasons,
> respects its great dynamics. She knows some of the
> deep grains and textures of the world because she
> knows some of the ways of its maker.
>
> —Cornelius Plantinga Jr. and Sue A. Rozeboom,
> *Discerning the Spirits: A Guide to Thinking
> about Christian Worship Today*

We now turn to the question of wisdom's relationship to everyday life. Much of history has treated wisdom as merely an idea, or some mass of information to be acquired by the mind. But biblical wisdom is far more than that. The link between wisdom and creation is foundational to a full understanding of biblical wisdom as it proves wisdom to be much more than intellectual fodder;

it is concerned with all of life—ordinary to extraordinary. This chapter introduces how wisdom is the clue to the Christian worldview and the importance of walking (not just knowing) God's wise way in his world.

Wisdom as a Totality Concept

In Al Wolters's classic book *Creation Regained,* he defines worldview as "the comprehensive framework of one's basic belief about things."[11] Regarding the need for a proper worldview, Wolters adds, "The need for a guiding perspective is basic to human life, perhaps more basic than food or sex."[12]

This need for a guiding perspective in life is where worldview and wisdom intersect. Let's return to Van Leeuwen's suggestion that wisdom is a "totality concept." He writes,

> [Wisdom] is as broad as reality and constitutes a culturally articulated way of relating to the entire world. The absence of wisdom is "folly," which like "wisdom" is expressed in a variety of Hebrew terms (Fox, *Proverbs*, 28–43). Thus, in the [Old Testament] good sailors, metalworkers, weavers, counselors, scribes, and builders—all may be described as "wise."[13]

Van Leeuwen further explains that wisdom was originally understood in relation to human craft, skill, and competence, and Old Testament wisdom literature did not abandon that notion. It did, however, reconceive wisdom in relation to Yahweh. Van Leeuwen writes, "Ancient wisdom thought and practice are never 'secular,' even where God is not mentioned. Thus, even farming is an aspect of religion (Isa 28:23–29)."[14]

As a totality concept, then, wisdom serves as our guiding perspective that brings God, the world, who we are as humans, and our role in God's world into clear focus. The application of wisdom should not be limited only to certain dimensions of life and reality. There is nothing secular (unrelated to God) in creation. Therefore, everything is within the scope of wisdom's purview, and Proverbs suggests that wisdom serves as the proper lens through which to view all of life—like putting on a pair of eyeglasses to see more clearly.

Wisdom and Creation

Van Leeuwen argues elsewhere that Proverbs 1–9 does not simply embody a worldview. It aims to "inculcate a particular Yahwistic worldview."[15] That is, Proverbs gives its readers a view of the world that corresponds to how God built it and how God intends for people to interact with it. The epigraph above from Plantinga and Rozeboom emphasizes this point. They add further,

> Wisdom is a reality-based phenomenon. To be wise is to know reality, to *discern* it. ... The discerning person notices the differences between things, but also the connections between them. She knows creation—what God has put together and what God has kept asunder—and can therefore spot the fractures and alloys introduced by human violation of it.[16]

Van Leeuwen, Plantinga, Rozeboom, and Wolters all highlight the role of creation in biblical wisdom. For many, wisdom remains merely an intellectual virtue that lives in the head but never affects the heart or hands. This, I fear, is a lingering influence from pagan Greek thought that prioritizes the mind over the rest of the human person.

Biblical wisdom is not so. Certainly, the mind plays a critical role in learning and understanding—both are dominant themes in Proverbs. But proper application of wisdom in all of life is the end goal—not just knowing. The skill of loving God and neighbor, upholding justice, knowing when and when not to speak, and the like are evidence of mature biblical wisdom in those who fear God and walk in his ways.

Thus, it is difficult to overstate the importance of wisdom's relation to creation. We must be careful not to exclude wisdom's relation to God and conflate the distinction between Creator and creation. God is the fount of true wisdom, and by this wisdom he "founded the earth" (Prov 3:19). As such, God, Christ, and creation are all integral and irreducible for a full understanding, acquisition, and application of biblical wisdom in the world.

Wisdom as the Clue to Christian Worldview

Putting on the lens of biblical wisdom brings all of life into clear focus and illumines God's ways in his world. As such, wisdom provides both clarity and coherence to life. It offers hope for those who fear the Lord, that we can walk with confidence in this life. There is a firm and principled foundation for those in leadership to lead with love, uphold justice, and extend honor and equity to all people. There is surety for parents to raise their children in the ways of the Lord. While Proverbs does not promise that children will remain faithful to God, it is clear that living according to God's way is the best way to live in his world and teaching this to our children is the most loving thing parents can do.

Moreover, if it is true that wisdom is a totality concept, which serves as a lens for life (or the clue to creation), then asking "What is wisdom's relationship to X?" should clarify the way of the Lord for that part of life and creation. For example, What is wisdom's way in finances? work? disciplining children? leadership? friendship? education?

This is precisely our approach in this study when considering the many ordinary themes that Proverbs discusses. Work, parenting, leadership, politics, money, sex, talking, listening, education—wisdom relates to all of it, all of life. Approaching Proverbs in this way avoids the piecemeal methods of a proverb a day, preferring instead a unified, coherent reading of the book as a whole and recognizing its place in the overarching story of the Bible.

For example, asking "What is wisdom's way with finances?" grounds one's approach in the core ingredients of wisdom discussed in chapter 2, then connects to the approximately seventy-three verses in Proverbs that deal with money.[17] These connections frame financial matters in relation to Yahweh and illumine the way of wisdom in contrast to the way of folly. And they do so in a way that keeps continuity with the whole of Proverbs and with the whole of Scripture.

In this view, nothing in creation is unrelated to wisdom. To the contrary, everything in creation comes into clear focus when viewed through the lens of wisdom. Wisdom is the clue to the Christian worldview—the proper lens through which creatures discern how to properly live in the Creator's world.

Walking the Wise Way

Our responsibility as Godfearers is to walk in wisdom's way in every time and place—for all times and places belong to God. What could be more ordinary in life than walking? Thus, what illustration could be more fitting for applying God's wisdom in daily life?

"Walking" appears more than 20 times in the book of Proverbs, and well over 300 times in the entire Bible. Proverbs is hardly alone in this emphasis. In Deuteronomy 10:12, Moses insists that what is most important to the Lord is to fear Him, love Him, and "walk in all his ways."[18] Psalm 1 illustrates the distinction between wisdom and folly, teaching that those who delight in the instruction of the Lord and reject the way of sinners are truly blessed. Further, Paul makes much of walking in his epistles as he insists that Christians "walk worthy" of the Lord (Col 1:10; Eph 4:1 HCSB).

Perhaps most significant is John 14:6, where Jesus declares that he is "the way, and the truth, and the life." By identifying as the "way," Jesus attaches this mega-theme to himself, and ultimately grounds the reality of the "way" in himself as God in the flesh. Jesus as "way" is just as significant as Jesus as "wisdom," for "way" identifies the proper boundaries and direction of wisdom.[19]

Walking in the way of wisdom is to live according to how God made us to live—in glad obedience to him, delighting in his law of love, keeping and cultivating his world to the praise of his glory. This direction of life promotes blessedness and flourishing for all people and signals to the world that God's way is best.

But how does this wise approach to life relate to the brokenness, hardship, and suffering that we experience? Could all this "wise way" business be too simplistic? Does it account for the ugliness we often encounter in the world?

"WALK" IN PROVERBS

In Proverbs, "walk" is usually a metaphor describing one's way of life:

> My child, do not walk in their way,
> keep your foot from their paths. (1:15)

> Therefore walk in the way of the good, and keep
> to the paths of the just. (2:20)

> Do not enter the path of the wicked,
> and do not walk in the way of evildoers. (4:14)

> Lay aside immaturity, and live,
> and walk in the way of insight. (9:6)

Each of these passages underscores the way of wisdom (in contrast to the way of folly) as perhaps the most dominant theme in Proverbs. Our responsibility as those who fear the Lord is to walk in wisdom's way and forsake folly.

Problem and Solution

Proverbs poses a problem. It poses many problems, in fact; but there is one problem greater than the rest that is in need of a solution. I'm not referring to authenticity concerns, doctrinal discrepancies, or interpretive issues (though Proverbs certainly contains its doctrinal and interpretive challenges); the chief problem I'm referring to is the problem of folly—the way of wickedness.

One might expect the problem of Proverbs simply to be labeled "sin"—the perennial problem of the biblical drama. And this is true. But in Proverbs, the problem is far more earthy than an abstract notion of sin. Folly is personal—a way of life, part of the ornery ordinary of our creaturely existence.

In the drama of Proverbs, Lady Folly plays a starring role as the adversary to the hero, Lady Wisdom. Folly and Wisdom each manifest in various forms throughout Proverbs and in other parts of Scripture. Perhaps most significant about them, though, is that they are two— for example, two trees (Gen 2; Ps 1; Prov 11), two women (Prov 7; 9), two ways (Ps 1; Prov 1). This tells us a few things about God's world.

1. God built choice into his world from the beginning and alerted Adam and Eve to it in the garden.

2. God built limits and boundaries into his world, as illustrated by moral boundaries made clear in the law, as well as by the boundaries between land and sea, heavens and earth.

3. Two ways of living—and only two ways—emerge from the limits and boundaries God built into his world. These two ways are most vividly illustrated in Proverbs as two women: Lady Wisdom and Lady Folly.

4. God built human responsibility into his world, and he calls people to obey him by walking in his ways.

The heart of the problem, though, is that humans are not good at walking in God's ways. Each of us carry the disease of sin, and thus folly comes naturally. We like it; we look for it; we invent it; indeed, we are addicted to it without realizing it; and—worst of all—we cannot stop it. "Like a dog that returns to its vomit, we revert to our folly" (Prov 26:11, adapted), for in it we find comfort, familiarity, and momentary pleasure. But this folly is not just playful mischief. It is an offense to God.

The solution is the beauty of the biblical drama. Jesus, the Wisdom of God, severs the cycle of human sin by outfoxing folly and breaking the very thing that broke God's world—sin and death. The good news of Jesus' life, death, and resurrection offers hope for foolish people. Believing in and being joined with Christ reorients one's life to begin in humility with the fear of the Lord, then to walk forever in the way of wisdom.

Walking this path of wisdom in everyday, ordinary life is the foil to folly. Though laziness may be appealing, wisdom insists, "Go to the ant, you lazybones," to see that hard work is best (Prov 6:6). While one may find a neighbor's wife attractive, wisdom asks, "Why should you be intoxicated ... by another woman and embrace the bosom of an adulteress?" (5:20). Instead, "Let your fountain be blessed, and rejoice in the wife of your youth" (5:18).

The gospel of Jesus heals human beings from the inside out, compelling us toward wisdom, our new and true addiction. Walking this way promotes the wisdom of God as the clue to life in God's world, the solution to sin and folly, and the way of life everlasting.

> **SUGGESTED READING**
> ☐ Proverbs 3:1–35
> ☐ Matthew 7:24–27

Reflection

Put into your own words how wisdom is the clue to the Christian worldview. How does wisdom connect to all of life?

_____

_____

_____

Consider how Christian wisdom unifies all of life. While Proverbs is sometimes read as a random book of tips for life, how are you beginning to see that walking in wisdom brings unity, coherence, and value to even the most ordinary activities?

_____

_____

_____

4

FEAR OF THE LORD

PROVERBS 1:1–7

Fear of the Lord is the cultivated awareness of the
"more and other" that the presence or revelation of God
introduces into our lives: I am not the center of my
existence; I am not the sum-total of what matters;
I don't know what will happen next.

—Eugene Peterson, *Christ Plays in Ten Thousand Places*

Perhaps the most awkward three days of my life were
college orientation. The annual tradition of orientation
and matriculation continues at my alma mater, Union
University, as it does at most academic institutions.
During these three days, the university's student life office
tries desperately to turn strangers into best friends, in
order to make the transition to college smoother. It's a
necessary part of early college life, I suppose, but it is
awkward, nonetheless.

Amid meeting people and making friends, students are
infused with the university's "core competencies." These
are the principles around which the school is formed, and

they are instilled into every student regardless of gender, race, nationality, or program of study. It's the part of the curriculum about which the university president insists, "If you don't get anything else during your time here, get these things."

The core competencies from Union have stuck with me over the years and continue to shape who I am. The aims of being "excellence-driven, Christ-centered, people-focused, and future-directed" are fundamental to my outlook on life.

When we open the book of Proverbs, we begin the orientation process for "Solomon's School of Wisdom." The opening verses align us to the book (indeed, to the world!), and they furnish its core competencies.

This chapter considers Proverbs 1:1–7 as the introduction to the book. We will briefly discuss the meaning of the four key infinitives found in verses 2–6, followed by sections on the fear of the Lord and the nature of wisdom as being more than intellectual.

Beginning in verse 2, the prologue reads,

> For **learning** about wisdom and instruction,
>   for **understanding** words of insight,
> for **gaining instruction** in wise dealing,
>   righteousness, justice, and equity;
> **to teach shrewdness** to the simple,
>   knowledge and prudence to the young—
> let the wise also hear and gain in learning,
>   and the discerning acquire a skill,
> **to understand** a proverb and a figure,
>   the words of the wise and their riddles.

> The fear of the LORD is the beginning of knowledge;
> fools despise wisdom and instruction.[20]

Various translations render the words differently (as shown on the following page), but all major translations identify four key terms (infinitives in Hebrew) in verses 2–6 that serve as the core competencies of Proverbs. The NRSV translates them as "learning," "understanding," "gaining instruction," and "teaching shrewdness." "Understanding" appears twice (1:2, 6). Let's briefly consider each of these terms.

Learning

It seems obvious to anyone seeking wisdom that "learning" (Hebrew: *yd'*) would be a basic part of the process. But why is learning basic to wisdom, and how does it inform our reading of Proverbs?

First, recall the emphasis on learning throughout the book. Following the theme verse (Prov 1:7), the author immediately returns to the parent-to-child voice of instruction in 1:8: "Hear, my child your father's instruction, and do not reject your mother's teaching." In other words, Proverbs avoids an apologetic for why learning is important. Instead, it assumes that anyone reading the book has taken the posture of a learner—one that resembles a child watching, listening, and learning from mom and dad.

This parent-to-child motif is important for several reasons: (1) it informs the way we transfer wisdom to younger generations (and how it was transferred to us); (2) it models the posture we should assume in relation to

Five Translations of Proverbs 1:2–7

NRSV	NASB95	NIV	HCSB	ESV
1:2 For learning about wisdom and instruction, for understanding words of insight,	1:2 To know wisdom and instruction, To discern the sayings of understanding,	1:2 for gaining wisdom and instruction; for understanding words of insight;	1:2 For learning what wisdom and discipline are; for understanding insightful sayings;	1:2 To know wisdom and instruction, to understand words of insight,
3 for gaining instruction in wise dealing, righteousness, justice, and equity;	3 To receive instruction in wise behavior, righteousness, justice and equity;	3 for receiving instruction in prudent behaviour, doing what is right and just and fair;	3 for receiving wise instruction in righteousness, justice, and integrity;	3 to receive instruction in wise dealing, in righteousness, justice and equity;
4 to teach shrewdness to the simple, knowledge and prudence to the young—	4 To give prudence to the naive, To the youth knowledge and discretion,	4 for giving prudence to those who are simple, knowledge and discretion to the young—	4 for teaching shrewdness to the inexperienced, knowledge and discretion to a young man—	4 to give prudence to the simple, knowledge and discretion to the youth—
5 let the wise also hear and gain in learning, and the discerning acquire skill,	5 A wise man will hear and increase in learning, And a man of understanding will acquire wise counsel,	5 let the wise listen and add to their learning, and let the discerning get guidance—	5 a wise man will listen and increase his learning, and a discerning man will obtain guidance—	5 Let the wise hear and increase in learning, and the one who understands obtain guidance,
6 to understand a proverb and a figure, the words of the wise and their riddles.	6 To understand a proverb and a figure, The words of the wise and their riddles.	6 for understanding proverbs and parables, the sayings and riddles of the wise.	6 for understanding a proverb or a parable, the words of the wise, and their riddles.	6 to understand a proverb and a saying, the words of the wise and their riddles.
7 The fear of the LORD is the beginning of knowledge; fools despise wisdom and instruction.	7 The fear of the LORD is the beginning of knowledge; fools despise wisdom and instruction.	7 The fear of the LORD is the beginning of knowledge, but fools despise wisdom and instruction.	7 The fear of the LORD is the beginning of knowledge; fools despise wisdom and discipline.	7 The fear of the LORD is the beginning of knowledge; fools despise wisdom and instruction.

God, our Father. Proverbs is an invitation to sit at wisdom's table, eating and drinking the stuff of life, love, justice, goodness, truth, and beauty, with explicit instructions for how we promote this way in our Father's world.

> "Fear-of-the-Lord is not studying about God but living in reverence before God."
>
> —Eugene Peterson, *Christ Plays in Ten Thousand Places*

Second, a posture of learning is a posture of humility. Humility is required not only for learning, but for all the core competencies, and especially for the fear of the Lord. Pride has no place at wisdom's table. The prideful have nothing to learn. They prefer to speak rather than listen, to make comments rather than ask questions. And in those instances when they are quiet, beware! They have not suddenly become wise; they are waiting for the perfect opportunity to pounce on the conversation with their oversimplified solution, convinced that their "wisdom" will answer all questions and solve all problems in one rhetorical fell swoop.

Understanding

"Understanding" (Hebrew: *bana*) appears twice in Proverbs' prologue (1:2, 6). The first appearance pertains to understanding "words of insight," and the second to understanding "a proverb and a figure" (or saying). The emphasis on understanding speaks to the importance of reflection and contemplation. The reflective person is one who, after learning (the first core competency), considers what has been taught. He reflects deeply and desires not merely to know, but to understand.

In both instances of the term, "understanding" portrays the activity of reflection and contemplation. Solomon was no doubt in the business of thoughtful reflection as a collector of proverbs from all over the world. The book of Proverbs is largely a collection of proverbs that, in Solomon's view, correspond with truth and how God designed the world. Recognizing this, however, from any given proverb does not happen immediately. A proverb, saying, or riddle requires reflection, and after much pondering the fog lifts and the matter becomes clear.

Gaining Instruction

For Proverbs, "gaining instruction" is directly related to the matter of "wise dealing"—how to behave in God's world. Wise dealing is characterized by three important terms: righteousness, justice, and equity.

Why does wisdom uphold righteousness, justice, and equity? Because these three attributes undergird what Jesus said is most important about living in God's world: loving God and loving others (Mark 12:29–31).

Gaining instruction in wise dealing does far more than fill our minds. It shapes our souls and activates our bodies to participate lovingly in God's world. In this way, pastors should promote righteousness, lenders should ensure equity, and politicians should uphold justice (to give a few examples). And this is but a taste of God's way in the world—a taste of his kingdom come on earth as it is in heaven.

Teaching Shrewdness

Proverbs 1:4 notes the importance of teaching "shrewdness to the simple, knowledge and prudence to the young." This core competency is unique, as it is immediately followed by a brief proverb that deepens and illustrates the point. Verse 5 states, "Let the wise also hear and gain in learning, and the discerning acquire skill."

The point is simple but profound, and imperative for anyone who desires wisdom: Wise people listen! And discerning people (people of understanding) are willing to learn.

Verse 4 focuses on the simple and young who have much to learn, especially regarding life experience. But verse 5 includes the mature, older people who, while they already may be considered wise, still have much to learn. Both verses 4 and 5 serve as a test for determining whether someone is wise. The test is this: Are you a good listener? Good listeners are generally teachable, and they demonstrate the humility necessary to gain wisdom. If someone is not a good listener, he has nothing to learn and is disinterested in wisdom.

On this point, Proverbs is unconcerned with age. While much of Proverbs models the transfer of wisdom from older to younger, a willingness to listen and learn is a prerequisite to gaining wisdom regardless of age or stage of life. Indeed, beyond merely learning, the wise person aims to understand. This requires more than just listening. The wise lean into a matter with sharp and thoughtful questions in order to truly understand. This is the attitude of those who consider the interests of others above their own, for by seeking to understand another's perspective, the wise person empties herself of her own opinions and self-interests—at least momentarily—in order to better inhabit the situation of the other. This requires genuine love and care for other people. Indeed, this requires loving one's neighbor as oneself.

Perhaps, most importantly, those who do not listen and learn not only neglect wisdom, they never even make it to the starting point.

The Starting Point: Fear of the Lord

The fear of the Lord (Yahweh) is the anthem of the book of Proverbs. It is the climax of the introduction, the dominant refrain throughout the book, and the capstone of the final chapter (31:30). The language of "fearing the Lord" appears approximately fourteen times throughout Proverbs, and it delineates major sections of the book (at 1:7; 9:10; 31:30), reinforcing its thrust at every turn.

But how should we understand "fear of the Lord"? And how does it relate to wisdom as prescribed in Proverbs? I find that the question of fearing God puzzles many Christians. Few people, in my experience, deny its importance; but few admit to having a clear grasp of what it means.

First, it is important to recognize fear of the Lord as both the threshold and bedrock for the way of wisdom. About this we need to consider two things.

Concerning fear of the Lord as a threshold, acquiring true wisdom begins with a proper view of God. Because wisdom is an attribute of God that he etched into his world at creation, understanding how to live wisely in God's world must begin with a healthy view of him. If the God of the Bible is the Creator of all things, then understanding and wisdom manifest when knowledge is properly ordered to him.

This brings to mind C. S. Lewis's quote: "I believe in Christianity as I believe that the Sun has risen, not only because I see it but because by it, I see everything else."[21] Knowledge that begins with a proper view of God—one that believes he is who he says he is, and that every created thing exists by, in, through, and for him—is knowledge that starts on the right foot and in the right direction. Does this mean that people who do not believe in the God of the Bible have no knowledge? Certainly not. It does mean, however, that without the fear of the Lord their knowledge begins in the wrong place and is therefore incomplete.

Tremper Longman says it well: "[The fear of the Lord] is the first thought that makes all other thoughts fall into place."[22] Without a proper view of God, particular pieces of knowledge cannot be understood in relation to the whole. Anyone can see what is on a single puzzle piece, but how can we understand the whole picture of the puzzle without seeing the front of the box? A proper view of God—and of oneself in relation to God—serves as the front of the puzzle box, showing how the pieces relate to the whole. The fear of the Lord is the starting point for seeing the whole picture and for accounting for all of reality.

Concerning fear of the Lord as the bedrock, then, this speaks to the overarching metaphor of "way" in Proverbs and throughout the whole of Scripture. The theme of the two ways (Hebrew: *derek*; Greek: *hodos*) is a mega-theme in the Bible that especially pertains to wisdom. Psalm 1, for example, opens the Psalter acknowledging the two ways: one way corresponds to wisdom and leads to flourishing; the other corresponds to folly and leads to ruin. The entire book of Proverbs can be summarized as such (without much oversimplification). Then it illumines the truth of this wisdom/folly duality in the ordinary activities of life (work, parenting, spending money, sleep, friendship, and so on).

Deuteronomy 10:12–13 is particularly important here. Bearing in mind the climactic role of Moses' words at this time and place in Israel's history adds even greater weight to this passage. Moses sets up his comments with a rhetorically pregnant question: "So now, O Israel, what does the LORD your God require of you?" Such a question should have put every Israelite on high alert as Moses prepared to summarize what matters most to God.

He answers, "Only to *fear* the LORD your God, to walk in all his *ways*, to love him, to serve the LORD your God with all your heart and with all your soul, and to keep the commandments of the LORD your God and his decrees that I am commanding you today, for your own well-being."

I added emphasis to the words "fear" and "ways" to highlight the connection between the two. The fear of the Lord serves as the bedrock, the firm foundation, for the way of the Lord. This way of living in God's world is what God intended for humans from the beginning. It is a way characterized by obedience to Yahweh, understanding oneself as a creature endowed with the image of the

Creator, worshiping him with all of one's life, and keeping and cultivating all of creation to promote the shalom and kingship of Yahweh over all time and space.

> "Effective knowledge about God is the only thing that puts a man into a right relationship with the objects of his perception."
>
> —Gerhard Von Rad, *Wisdom in Israel*

This way is the best way of living because it was designed by God. It is the way of life, love, truth, goodness, beauty, justice, and anything else that speaks of the goodness of our God. And it begins with the fear of the Lord.

Secondly, it is important to recognize the multifaceted nature of "fear" in the "fear of the Lord." I often hear the question, "Does 'fear of the Lord' mean that I should be afraid of God?" Perhaps more precisely we should consider if "terror," or something similar, is what "fear of the Lord" means? The answer is both yes and no.

The Hebrew word for "fear," *yir'a(h)*, carries the ideas of terror and respect/reverence/awe. Thus, Godfearers should maintain a healthy sense of the terror of God. He is not one to be crossed, questioned, or disobeyed. I recall the genuine terror I felt as a kid when I deliberately disobeyed my father. He was right and just to be angry with me, and it is not a stretch to say that terror seized my soul—and since my dad is 6'5" and 270 pounds with red hair, who wouldn't be scared?

In a similar fashion, we should respect who God is and obey his commands. Failure to do so should frighten us at the deepest part of our being. With the author of

Ecclesiastes, we declare, "God is in heaven, and [we] upon earth; therefore let [our] words be few" (Eccl 5:2b).

The other angle of *yir'a(h)* speaks to the gentler side of fear. This is the deep and abiding reverence we have for God, reminiscent of Isaiah when he "saw the Lord ... high and lifted up" (Isa 6:1 ESV), and of Peter when he first met Jesus in Luke 5. To live a Godfearing life means nothing less than a life that promotes reverence for God and his way in the world. This is far more than lip service and church attendance. This is all of life! Ours is the God of all space and time, not merely of church buildings and Sunday mornings. The fear of the Lord reinforces this to us at every moment, keeping we, the creatures, in awe of him, the Creator.

As Eugene Peterson says so well, "The moment we find ourselves unexpectedly in the presence of the sacred, our first response is to stop in silence. We do nothing. We say nothing. We fear to trespass inadvertently; we are afraid of saying something inappropriate. Plunged into mystery we become still, we fall silent, all our senses alert. This is the fear-of-the-Lord."[23]

Finally, the fear of the Lord is a matter of faith. With Henri Blocher, I would argue that the Old Testament notion of the fear of the Lord is equivalent to the New Testament notion of faith.[24] When we begin at the proper starting point—rightly aligning ourselves to God and recognizing him for who he is as the great "I Am" and Creator of all things—then all knowledge, experience, perception, and relationships begin to fall into place. In this way, the fear of the Lord functions as a confession of faith upon which we fix our foundation and from which we take directions.

Is Wisdom Merely Intellectual?

In a recent lecture on intellectual renewal for the church, Rowan Williams commented that many people assume "intellectual" to mean "detached from reality." "An intellectual," Williams notes, "does not know how to boil an egg, but will write a treatise on the subject for you."[25] Instead, Williams argues that we need to recover the original meaning of the word "intellectual." The clue, he says, is in the Latin root, *intus*, meaning "within" or "on the inside." In other words, Williams suggests that an intellectual should seek to "get inside the skin" of an issue or thing being considered.

This sounds to me quite like the nature of wisdom. Getting inside the skin of something is quite the opposite of detached. Certainly, there is a cerebral dimension to being intellectual, but if it remains in the head and never moves to the heart and hands, it falls short of the true meaning of *intus*. Likewise, when humans acquire knowledge, but that knowledge fails to mature to understanding and proper application, it falls short of wisdom.

In the spirit of Proverbs, the wise person is not some detached intellectual. Instead, she is a complete human being who seeks to get into the skin of—that is, to fully understand from the inside out—whatever she is considering. This may be a new area of study such as economics or biology. Or it might be the experience of a Holocaust survivor, an abandoned child, or the pressures of a world leader. In any case, the wise person aims her intellect into the guts of the matter to understand as best she can. And only afterward does she allow her opinions and judgments to form.

Approaching life in this way respects the complexities of human experience. Too often, we are slow to listen, quick to speak, and quick to anger (Jas 1:19) as our opinions form about people and situations. This tends to render quick and ill-informed judgments on complicated issues in life. It oversimplifies the facts and fails (even refuses) to see things from another's perspective.

Yet, wisdom calls for us to be "quick to listen, slow to speak, and slow to anger" (Jas 1:19). This means that wisdom requires more than a sharp mind. It engages the whole person—head, heart, and hands—to embody love, patience, and self-control. If this is neglected, people become strangely less than human, less than imagers of God.

When attending only to the mind, humans devolve into stale encyclopedias of detached data, lacking coherence and integration of thought and falling short of understanding and proper application. When attending only to the heart, humans morph into bags of mindless emotion and empathy without root or rudder for discerning and promoting love, truth, and justice. When attending only to the hands, humans mutate into machines bent on production and utility with no place for wonder and beauty, and all of life is judged by the cost-benefit analysis.

The wise person is patient, understanding, and compassionate. He listens long to the struggles of a friend and suffers with them. She discerns when and what to speak in the moment that promotes the way of wisdom in specific situations. He sees beauty in ashes and remembers God's faithfulness in the past so as to live confidently in the future. She does not fear bad news, for her heart is firm in the Lord (Ps 112:6–8). Nor does she fear the opinions of others, as these are overshadowed by the fear of God. This way of life cares for neighbors, deals generously with those in need, considers the poor and the interests of others, works hard, rests often, and respects the creation that God has given us to steward. Indeed, this is *the* way of life.

"The glory of God is a living [human being]; and the life of [a human being] consists in beholding God," wrote St. Irenaeus, bishop of Lyons during the second century.[26] The human being who is fully alive has first been made alive by faith in the resurrected Christ. Then, filled with the living Spirit of God, we join with Christ—the Wisdom of God—walking along the way of wisdom that gives life to all who heed its call, and that promotes the ways of God in his world.

SUGGESTED READING

☐ Proverbs 1:1–33

☐ Psalm 111:1–10

Reflection

Consider the difference between "learning" and "understanding." How would you explain this in your own words, and how does it relate to being wise?

_____

_____

_____

How does wisdom relate to the Great Commandment of loving God and loving your neighbor?

_____

_____

_____

How would you describe the "fear of the Lord"? Where is proper God-fear lacking in your life, and where do you see it at work in your life?

_____

_____

_____

_____

5

WISDOM, CREATION, AND CHRIST

PROVERBS 8

Jesus Christ *is* our God-given wisdom ...
and he *enables* us to become wise as we have
his mind by the Spirit.

—Daniel J. Treier, "Wisdom" in *Dictionary of Theological
Interpretation of the Bible*

We now turn to the important intersection of wisdom, creation, and Christ, especially as it is presented in Proverbs 8. Proverbs 8:22–31 was the source of substantial theological debate in the early fourth century, leading to the first ecumenical council of the church in AD 325. And, while the dust has long settled between Arius, Alexander, and Athanasius, there is still room for various interpretations of Proverbs 8 concerning Christ.

In this chapter, we do not aim to answer every question about Christ in relation to Proverbs 8. Rather we gladly invoke the language of the Nicene Creed concerning

the relationship between the Father and the Son, that
Christ is:

> the only-begotten Son of God
> begotten of the Father before all ages,
> Light of Light
> true God of true God,
> begotten, not made;
> of one substance with the Father
> through whom all things were made.[27]

This language from the creed underscores wisdom, creation, and Christ as mega-themes in Scripture that come
together in Proverbs, offering interpretive handles for
navigating this important passage.

Wisdom as Christ in Proverbs

Though Proverbs predates the birth of Christ by several
hundred years,[28] we must not forget that, ultimately,
wisdom culminates in the person of Jesus. Several New
Testament passages alert us to the integral link between
Jesus and wisdom. He is "the power of God and the wisdom
of God" (1 Cor 1:24; see also 12:8) and the one "in whom
are hidden all the treasures of wisdom and knowledge"
(Col 2:3).

How then does this affect the way we read Proverbs?
While opinions abound, we approach Proverbs with
Christ at the center of our interpretive lens—the Wisdom
of God who walked perfectly in the way of the Lord and
who is the Way of the Lord (John 14:6). Jesus is the perfect
Wisdom that comes down from above; that is "first pure,
then peaceable, gentle, willing to yield, full of mercy and

good fruits, without a trace of partiality or hypocrisy" (Jas 3:17).

Jesus' life illustrates the wisdom of Proverbs, as he modeled wisdom's way on earth in the flesh. He lived out the way of God in the world as child, son, brother, carpenter, friend—indeed, as the Christ. Moreover, his sacrificial death for sinners followed by his victorious resurrection enthroned the carpenter from Nazareth as the King of creation who calls his people to walk in his way. This Jesus is no mere man. He is God, and therefore he shares in the divine nature of the God who is three and one. And wisdom is an expression of this divine nature.

In the incarnate Christ we behold the Wisdom of God. He is the one in whom "all the fullness of God was pleased to dwell" (Col 1:19a) in bodily form. The Creator became creation (though, not creature), and through him all of creation is being healed, beginning with those who believe in Jesus. As Christ's followers walk in his way all over the world, we promote God's way of life in Jesus and we join him in giving life to the world (John 6:33). Thus, our lives align with how Jesus taught us to pray to the Father: "Your kingdom come. Your will be done, on earth as it is in heaven" (Matt 6:10).

Returning then to the question of interpretation, our approach suggests two things. First, approach Proverbs remembering Christ, the Wisdom of God. And, second, approach Proverbs recognizing the culmination of wisdom's way in Jesus in every passage of the book. This agrees with Jesus' teaching in John 5 and Luke 24 that the Scriptures testify to him. This does not necessarily make Proverbs messianic or prophetic in the same way as other parts of Scripture, but neither does it ignore the central expression of wisdom in Scripture—Jesus himself.

Jesus' mission reestablishes wisdom—the way of God— in his world. This especially highlights the redeeming and restoring aspects of Jesus' life and ministry on earth.

CHRISTOCENTRIC AND CHRISTOTELIC READINGS OF PROVERBS

Is our reading of Proverbs "Christocentric"—that is, a reading that puts Christ at the center? Yes, in a sense, though it avoids narrowing the scope of the text and making Jesus the exclusive meaning of every verse. Is this reading of Proverbs "Christotelic"—one that sees Christ as the ultimate goal of each passage? Perhaps, in that we remember and recognize Jesus as the culmination of wisdom, both in its essence and in its function of living faithfully before God. However, it is not Christotelic in a prophetic sense. Jesus is the culmination of wisdom, but he is not the fulfillment of wisdom in the same way that he is the fulfillment or end (Greek: *telos*) of the law (Rom 10:4). Jesus is the second Adam, who has reclaimed and restored what the first Adam lost and allowed to be distorted by sin.

Proverbs 8:22–31

Who then is the mysterious person self-identified as Wisdom in Proverbs 8? The one who "lives with prudence" (8:12); the one who has good advice, insight, and strength (8:14); the one by whom "kings reign" and "rulers rule" (8:15, 16); the one who "walk[s] in the way of righteousness, along the paths of justice" (8:20)?

We might offer that the obvious answer is Jesus. The author of Proverbs doesn't make it that simple, however. Beginning in verse 22, we read:

> The LORD created me at the beginning of his work,
>   the first of his acts of long ago.

Simply equating Jesus with this personified Wisdom (a female figure) potentially renders Christ a created being. This is the famous Arian heresy condemned by the church in the early fourth century.

So how should we understand the person of Wisdom in Proverbs 8? After all, she seems to boast some of the same attributes that Christians attach to Jesus—namely, the first (or firstborn) of creation, with God from the beginning before anything was made, and the means by which all things were created.

Whatever conclusion one draws about this passage, at least three things are certain. First, there is an integral (albeit mysterious) relationship between Wisdom, creation, and Jesus. Second, both Wisdom and the Son—the Word (Greek: *logos*) of God—existed with God before anything else in creation was brought forth. Thirdly, there is some distinction between Wisdom, Jesus, and God the Father. While they may be related, they are not exactly the same at every point.

In his commentary on Proverbs, Daniel Treier offers a helpful approach to this passage. First, he suggests that the Hebrew word *qanah* in verse 22 is best translated "acquired" or "begot," and not "created."[29] This small but critical point alleviates much angst for Christian readings of this passage.

Secondly, Treier emphasizes the importance of remembering that this passage is poetry. He writes, "Metaphorical uses are frequent for the concept of creation in scripture, and after all this text is poetry."[30] As such, we need not hold it to the same literal standards of meaning that might be applied to direct, didactic portions of Scripture.

Thirdly, Treier turns to Philippians 2:5–11 as an important link that illumines the mystery of Proverbs 8:22–31. "Wisdom is the way God has made for humans to walk," Treier insists, and "Philippians 2:5 states the goal of wisdom, 'Let the same mind be in you that was in Christ Jesus.'" Treier continues,

> Philippians 2:6–11 points to the divine source of Wisdom by narrating its vocational shape in Jesus Christ: first descent, then ascent; humiliation before exaltation. Humans softly echo the crescendo of divine condescension, but Paul's appeal in Philippians works precisely because in Jesus we see *divine* condescension. ... Philippians 2 narrates the incarnation; Prov. 8 does not. Yet Phil. 2 has parallel logic, insofar as wisdom requires *both* divine condescension *and* human form for us to attain.[31]

Fourthly, Treier argues that "Jesus Christ therefore does not finally complicate the interpretation of Prov. 8 but presents instead the resolution of a mystery latent in the text, though not always clearly recognized."[32]

Finally, Treier offers St. Athanasius's perspective on Proverbs 8:22–31 that "correctly recognized the problematic character" of the Arian interpretation, which treated the Son of God as a creature instead of Creator.[33] Treier's concluding thoughts are worth considering at length:

> Interpreting Prov. 8 as having Christological relevance helps to hold together creation and redemption rather than prioritizing either in lopsided fashion. ... In Christ God confronts us with true Wisdom that is personal and redemptive, entailing response to divine initiative. Covenant life means the renewal of creation, while creaturely life is ultimately designed for covenant fellowship with God. ...
>
> Thus 8:31 comes alive in light of Jesus Christ. ... Jesus Christ endured the cross for the joy set before him (Heb. 12:1–2), because of God's commitment to creation and particularly to humans who bear the divine image. This Son shares the Father's character, so that by grace we might do so in turn.[34]

Thus, we end as we began. There is an integral, though mysterious, relationship between Wisdom, creation, and Jesus. We need not seek to untangle the theological knot of Proverbs 8:22–31 with too much precision. As Treier reminds us, it is a poetic passage that aims to underscore the integral relationship between Wisdom and creation. Proverbs 8 offers a resounding retort to Job's stunned silence at the Lord's interrogation of him in Job 38–41.

While Job can only confess that he "uttered what I did not understand" with respect to the counsel of the Lord and creation of all things (Job 42:3), the one called Wisdom can exclaim "I was there" when the Lord established the heavens and drew a circle on the face of the deep (Prov 8:27). [35]

SUGGESTED READING

☐ Proverbs 8:1–36

☐ 1 Corinthians 1:18–25

☐ Colossians 1:15–2:3

Reflection

Consider why the genre of a passage matters for inter-pretation. How might poetry (such as that found in Prov 8) be interpreted differently than historical books (such as Acts) or letters (such as Romans)?

_____

_____

_____

_____

Without making every word of Proverbs about Jesus, how does remembering and recognizing Jesus as the "power and wisdom of God" (1 Cor 1:24) clarify Proverbs for you?

_____

_____

_____

_____

_____

Articulate in your own words the relationship between Wisdom, creation, and Christ. What have Christ and Wisdom to do with creation? How does this affect how you live as a creature in God's world?

_____

_____

_____

_____

_____

6

TWO WOMEN
AND TWO WAYS

PROVERBS 9

With whom will we dine? Will we dine with
Woman Wisdom, who represents Yahweh's wisdom,
even Yahweh himself? Or will we dine with
Woman Folly, who represents the false gods
of the surrounding nations?

—Tremper Longman III, *Proverbs*

Women play a prominent role in Proverbs. In fact, Lady
Wisdom holds pride of place above any other character
in the book. Suffice it to say, the book of Proverbs is ade-
quately summarized as being about her and her ways in
God's world.

There is another woman, however, who also receives
much attention in Proverbs—Lady Folly. Lady Folly
opposes Lady Wisdom at every point and uses her

seductive beauty and charm to recruit both men and women to walk in her foolish way instead of Lady Wisdom's way.

This two-way theme features prominently throughout the book of Proverbs, as we have seen in previous chapters. But nowhere is it more on display than in Proverbs 9.

Here we arrive at the crossroads of Proverbs, strategically placed to call readers to decide which way they will walk. Like the theme of way, the theme of walking features prominently throughout the Old and New Testaments and is often found in context with way (or directional) language. This most ordinary activity of walking becomes a vivid and relatable illustration of the good life with God that calls Godfearers to walk in his ways, thereby promoting his ways throughout his world. As the title of this book suggests, Proverbs teaches us to walk in God's ways.

As we begin in Proverbs 9, what do we learn about Lady Wisdom? At least two major observations stand out regarding this extraordinary woman.

Lady Wisdom Works Hard

In the first two verses, Lady Wisdom builds her house, hews her seven pillars, slaughters her beasts, mixes her wine, and sets her table all in preparation for her invited guests (Prov 9:1–10). For some of us, just reading the previous sentence was exhausting! This woman is not afraid of hard work. She is handy to have around the house. She is crafty, and understands both the value of hard work and the how-to of skilled labor.

All of this teaches us about the nature of wisdom, the human role of work, and how wisdom and work intersect strategically in God's world as he intended. We will consider this further in the following chapters. For now, we recognize that Lady Wisdom's character is not laziness, but diligence. She does not sit around wasting time. She works hard. And, in this specific instance, her work is for the benefit of her guests.

Lady Wisdom is hospitable and generous. Five different verbs—builds, hews, slaughters, mixes, and sets—describe Lady Wisdom's preparation for those who will come and eat of her bread, and drink of her wine (Prov 9:5). Any one of these physical activities is enough to exhaust the hardest worker. And most, I suspect, would hardly exert such energies for anyone other than oneself and one's family.

Lady Wisdom selflessly and tirelessly prepares for her guests. All her activity is in the service of another. She bends her life toward the benefit of other people. She prioritizes her activities in preparation to give to those who visit her house. Sound familiar? Indeed, God has done precisely this for his people, especially in the person of his Son, Jesus.

Just as the Architect of all things taught that loving God and loving others is the most important law for living in his world (Mark 12), so Lady Wisdom orders all her life in like fashion. She considers others' interests above her own. She directs her love away from self and toward God and others. In other words, she walks—indeed, works!—wisdom's way.

Lady Wisdom Recruits for Righteousness and Gives Life

Following her work in verses 1-2, Lady Wisdom dispatches her servant girls to the "highest places in town." As Bruce Waltke observes concerning verse 3, "*She has sent out ...* entails that the banquet is now ready," and Lady Wisdom's servants function themselves like wisdom teachers on an "educational mission," inviting those who will hear to attend Wisdom's school—as opposed to Lady Folly, whose mission is seductive and sinful, inviting those who will hear to her bedroom.[36]

We must note the significance of Wisdom calling out from the "highest places in the town." Why not call out at the temple? Wouldn't it make sense to recruit in the place most dedicated to spiritual matters? Indeed, the place where God dwells? Wouldn't the top recruits be found there?

Wisdom's call does include the temple, I would argue, but it is not limited to the temple. The highest place in the town encompasses every place—the city center, the market, theaters, homes, the blacksmith's barn, the cabinet shop, banks, schools, hardware stores, restaurants, and places of worship. In other words, Wisdom calls to all places!

So, to whom is Wisdom's call addressed? Men? Women? Children? Americans? Africans? Asians? The answer is yes to all!

This call does not discriminate along gender, racial, or geopolitical lines. Nor is this call limited to certain times or places. "Wisdom is a totality concept," and her address applies to all times, places, and peoples.[37] As Waltke further observes, "The metaphor again dramatizes the truth that *wisdom pertains to all and to the life of the city* (see 1:20–21 and 8:1–4), and the repetition of this setting in the exposition of the stupid woman shows that she vies with her to win over the gullible (see 9:14)."[38]

The book of Proverbs assumes that all people image God in his world; we are co-regents responsible for walking in God's ways at all times and in all places. We proclaim the glory of the Creator and promote love for God and neighbor in all the earth. As such, our humanness is bound up in both our creatureliness (utter dependence upon the Creator) and in the fact that we are both body and soul, material and immaterial, seen and unseen. For too long, Christians have assumed that our bodies are, at best, secondary to our existence and, at worst, unnecessary.

The biblical witness, however, teaches that we were built with bodies on purpose. We experience God's world in its fullness as both body and soul. There is much more we could explore here, but the purpose is to highlight the link between wisdom and human beings. While the whole of creation reflects the wisdom of God, Lady Wisdom—indeed, God himself—expects his imagers to keep and cultivate his ways in his world.

While sin has corrupted, perverted, and misdirected God's good world, it has not rendered the creation bad.

Wisdom lived out by Godfearers echoes Lady Wisdom by uttering truth, displaying righteousness, and illuminating straight paths with our everyday lives.

Both Proverbs 8 and 9 call out to the "simple"—literally, the naive, those who are immature and usually young in age. For those who fit this description on the surface, sit up straight and prepare to learn. For those who believe themselves neither simple nor young, and thus assume Lady Wisdom's address is for another, you too would do well to sit up straight and prepare to be taught, for as verse 9 teaches, "Give instruction to the wise, and they will become wiser still; teach the righteous and they will gain in learning."

What does Wisdom teach to those who heed her call? All of Proverbs (indeed, all of the Bible) answers this question. But 9:5-10 offers a peek into the depth of Wisdom's ways. She begins by promising life to those who "eat her bread and drink her wine." This is evangelism, inviting those who have not heard to listen to the message of life:

Come, eat of my bread
  and drink of the wine I have mixed.
Lay aside immaturity, and live,
  and walk in the way of insight. (9:5-6)

The Promise of Life

The promise of life is a serious claim. Throughout the Bible, life is given by the Triune God (Father, Son, and Spirit) and the Scriptures themselves (the words of God). What does it mean to give life? For our purposes here, life given by wisdom is that which enables creatures to live according to their created purpose—to walk in God's ways.

As St. Irenaeus brilliantly asserted, "the glory of God is the human being fully alive."[39] This sentiment resonates deeply with Lady Wisdom's invitation to eat and drink from her table. Further, this all resonates deeply with John 6, where Jesus insists that he has come to give life to the world.

Hear Jesus' words from John 6:33–35 and 51–56:

> "For the bread of God is that which comes down from heaven and gives life to the world." They said to him, "Sir, give us this bread always."
>
> Jesus said to them, "I am the bread of life. Whoever comes to me will never be hungry, and whoever believes in me will never be thirsty. ...
>
> "I am the living bread that came down from heaven. Whoever eats of this bread will live forever; and the bread that I will give for the life of the world is my flesh." ... So Jesus said to them, "Very truly, I tell you, unless you eat the flesh of the Son of Man and drink his blood, you have no life in you. Those who eat my flesh and drink my blood have eternal life, and I will raise them up on the last day; for my flesh is true food and my blood is true drink. Those who eat my flesh and drink my blood abide in me, and I in them."

These words from Christ are among the most profound in all the New Testament. And these verses have served as the center of much controversy through the centuries regarding how Christians understand the Eucharist (the Lord's Supper). We will not address Eucharistic practices here, but we must highlight the connection between Lady Wisdom's invitation to eat and drink from her table and Jesus' invitation to eat and drink of himself. Both give life!

Wisdom's plea is to eat and drink of Christ. He is the bread that fills and the wine that satisfies. And in this eating—another most ordinary, yet necessary human activity—we ingest eternal life. The food that is Christ is not temporary like all other food. While wholesome meals that provide energy and nutrients to our current bodies will sustain us for a few hours until we need more, the food of Christ nourishes for eternity.

While talking with a friend and mentor some years ago, I asked his opinion on the meaning and definition of discipleship in the Christian life. He answered, "Discipleship is teaching people to eat and drink Jesus." Honestly, my immediate thought was, "That's the strangest thing I've ever heard." But the more I chewed on it, the more the truth of his statement resonated deep within and illumined the words of Scripture.

Both Lady Wisdom and Jesus call forth the same invitation to the world: come, eat and drink of me, for in me is life and the way of life, both now and forever. Just as Hebrews 6 informs us that Christ is our eternal priest, Proverbs 9 insists that Christ—the Wisdom of God—is our eternal feast. After all, we are what we eat.[40]

The Beginning of Knowledge and Wisdom

"The fear of the LORD is the beginning of wisdom, and the knowledge of the Holy One is insight" (Prov 9:10). Following examples of wise sayings in verses 7–9, the author reminds the reader where wisdom begins: with the fear of the Lord. Verse 10 serves as an *inclusio* that began with 1:7—"The fear of the LORD is the beginning of knowledge"—and now ends with "The fear of the LORD is the beginning of wisdom."[41] Most understand "knowledge" and "wisdom" as essentially synonyms describing the same idea. While there is certainly some conceptual overlap, there are also important distinctions to notice.

Consider the nature of knowledge, then consider wisdom. One can have knowledge without wisdom, but not wisdom without knowledge. As such, they are related, but not quite the same. Knowledge is more basic—a building block of sorts that can be ordered toward wisdom. But knowledge—even of the most sophisticated sort—can also be ordered toward foolishness. Indeed, some of the most infamous criminals in history were remarkably smart, even shrewd, and possibly prudent—but not wise.

The point is that the fear of the Lord is the starting point for both knowledge and wisdom. The author starts with knowledge, and nine chapters later reinforces the proper starting point by referring not to knowledge, but to the more mature idea of wisdom—the very thing humans should aim for in the first place. Knowledge is not the goal; wisdom is, for wisdom is that attribute of God that is woven into creation, ordering all things according to God's ways. And Godfearers are responsible for promoting this way in God's world.

The Contrast between Wisdom and Folly

The stark contrast between Lady Wisdom and Lady Folly shocks readers into recognizing the severity of this alternative way called foolishness. One immediately observes that, unlike Lady Wisdom, Lady Folly is described as loud, ignorant, and lazy (9:13–18). Whereas Lady Wisdom was slow to speak, full of knowledge and understanding, and hardworking, Lady Folly promotes a competing way of life—a lifestyle characterized by obnoxiousness, noisiness, an abundance of words with no wisdom, and vain busyness without meaningful service to the world.

Lady Wisdom	Lady Folly
• Begins with the fear of the Lord	• Begins with boisterousness
• Hard worker	• Lazy
• Gives from what is hers	• Steals and hides
• Serves others	• Self-serving
• Pleads to forsake folly and receive life (evangelism)	• Ends in destruction and death
• Teaches wisdom (discipleship)	• Teaches deception

Such people are not difficult to spot. No doubt, several have come to mind for you and me as we considered the last few sentences. And, yet, two things tend to be true for all of us. First, we despise foolish people like those described above. And, second, far too often, we are the foolish person described above.

When we speak about things we do not understand—be they political, theological, mechanical, financial, parental, personal, etc.—we promote the way of folly in God's world. When we neglect to work hard out of love for God and for the benefit of others, we not only promote but participate in the way of folly. When we forsake the gift of meekness and thoughtful exhortation of others in favor of gaining attention, we embody Lady Folly.

In many cases, such instances in our lives may seem innocent enough; and I am not suggesting that every instance is a matter of straightforward sin. Sometimes this is the case, but at other times it is simply a preference for the way of folly over the way of wisdom. Like Wisdom, Lady Folly is in the recruiting business. An important difference, however, is that Lady Folly recruits not *for* righteousness like Lady Wisdom, but *from* righteousness and for foolishness.

Proverbs 9:15 teaches that Lady Folly calls out "to those who pass by, who are going straight on their way." She is recruiting those walking "straight" (or righteously) to turn toward her way instead. Michael Fox observes, "Idioms meaning 'going straight' always connote moral virtue. This implies that the passerby whom Folly hopes to ensnare is not the wicked, who, after all, require no further enticement. Folly calls to ordinary people who are going about their business and are presumed honest. She hopes to sidetrack some gullible and witless souls among them."[42]

Listen Long!

Arguably, the most frightening feature of Proverbs 9 is the moment Lady Folly begins to speak. Why? Because, at first, her voice is identical to Lady Wisdom's.

> Verse 4 reads, "'You that are simple, turn in here!' To those without sense she says ..."

> Verse 16 reads, "'You who are simple, turn in here!' And to those without sense she says ..."

Which is Wisdom, and which is Folly?

This is terrifying for those who truly desire wisdom. And our daily lives correspond to this; sometimes it is difficult to discern the way of wisdom versus the way of folly. Whom to marry? Which job to pursue? Buy or rent? Whom to vote for? Millions of life decisions must be weighed daily, some of greater significance than others, but all informed by our tendencies toward either wisdom or folly.

This alerts us to the rest of the book of Proverbs. Beginning in chapter 10, the genre shifts from primarily prose that instructs about the nature of wisdom to sayings that illustrate Wisdom's way in the world in contrast to Folly's way. But how do we know which voice to listen to in moments of decision? The answer is that we must listen long. Just as Paul lists "longsuffering" (or patience) among the fruits of the Spirit in Galatians 5, so too should we be "long-listening" when making decisions in life.[43]

To listen long echoes James' instruction in James 1:19b: "Let everyone be quick to listen, slow to speak, and slow to anger." This further resonates with Proverbs 2:1-2, 5: "My child, if you accept my words and treasure up my commandments within you, making your ear attentive to wisdom and inclining your heart to understanding ... then you will understand the fear of the LORD and find the knowledge of God."

Listening is not the sole requirement for wisdom, however. The wise person begins by listening, carefully discerning Wisdom's voice as she cries out from on high in every time and place. But then the wise person must act in accordance with Wisdom's voice promoting God's ways, so that "your way may be known upon earth, your saving power among all nations" (Ps 67:2 ESV). This, too, echoes James 1 as he continues,

> But be doers of the word, and not merely hearers who deceive themselves. For if any are hearers of the word and not doers, they are like those who look at themselves in a mirror; for they look at themselves and, on going away, immediately forget what they were like. But those who look into the perfect law, the law of liberty, and persevere, being not hearers who forget but doers who act—they will be blessed in their doing. (Jas 1:22–25)

The Food of Death

The final verses from Proverbs 9:10–23 describe the feast of Lady Folly. In contrast to the life-giving feast from Wisdom's table, Folly's food promises pleasure and satisfaction but instead produces death.

Throughout this poetic section, one almost hears the sultry, seductive tone in Folly's voice as she lures the righteous from their straight path. Proverbs 7:10–23 adds to our imagination of Lady Folly's seductive recruiting techniques by telling the story, presumably narrated by Lady Wisdom, of the prostitute-like woman who lures young people to her home.

Passages like these should nauseate those who desire wisdom. Indeed, the metaphor is fitting here as readers are left to consider their appetites. Does our appetite favor the feast of Wisdom or Folly? The two invitations sound similar in the beginning, but after listening longer, the wise can discern that Wisdom's food was prepared from scratch out of her abundance, generously offered to those who will hear, and with life eternal baked into the meal.

Folly's food is stolen, accompanied by noisy know-it-alls who insist the water is sweet and bread is to die for. And, indeed, death is served for dessert.

We conclude then by asking, which way do you walk? Whose voice are you listening to and obeying? What food are you eating? Are you living or dying? As Lady Wisdom concludes in Proverbs 7,

> And now, my children, listen to me,
>> and be attentive to the words of my mouth.
> Do not let your hearts turn aside to her ways;
>> do not stray into her paths.
> For many are those she has laid low,
>> and numerous are her victims.
> Her house is the way to Sheol,
>> going down to the chambers of death. (7:24–27)

SUGGESTED READING

☐ Proverbs 9:1–18

☐ Psalm 1:1–6

Reflection

What is the difference between knowledge and wisdom? How are they related but different?

_____

_____

_____

Can you recall a time when you weren't sure which was the wise way and which was the foolish way? How did you decide, and was "listening long" part of the process?

_____

_____

_____

Does your life align more with the character of Lady Wisdom or Lady Folly? Why is that? Identify one thing you can do today to begin cultivating Lady Wisdom's character in your everyday life.

_____

_____

_____

7

THE WISE WOMAN AND MAN

PROVERBS 31:10–31

Neither women nor men are to be cherished for physical beauty alone; their deepest worth is in their capacity to embody wisdom.

—Craig G. Bartholomew and Ryan P. O'Dowd,
Old Testament Wisdom Literature

It is only fitting for the book of Proverbs to conclude with a hymn about the wise woman. Bartholomew and O'Dowd write, "Women, wives and wisdom constitute the central grain of Proverbs 1–9, giving these chapters the liminal urgency young men should feel for finding and loving wisdom."[44] An ode to this woman provides the perfect bookend to Proverbs as it furthers our understanding and appreciation for her, and connects wisdom more deeply with our ordinary lives.

Whereas the author of Proverbs speaks of Lady Wisdom and Lady Folly in the abstract by way of personification, now the author illustrates the way of wisdom with an actual wise woman (I like to think of her as "Sophie").

The present chapter will consist of two major sections: wisdom the woman and wisdom the human. In the first section, we will consider what the text teaches specifically concerning the wise woman, giving attention to her various vocations and activities that are wisely undertaken, all of which flow from her fear of the LORD (31:30).[45] This section especially appreciates wisdom as a woman—a woman who is wise in every respect, and who serves as the sapiential hero for both Jewish and Christian traditions. The second section will reflect on what the hymn teaches all people, irrespective of gender, race, ethnicity, social status, or geographical location.

Wisdom the Woman

The hymn to the wise woman found in Proverbs 31:10–31 is organized as an acrostic Hebrew poem, meaning that the first line of the poem begins with the first letter in the Hebrew alphabet (*aleph*), with each subsequent line beginning with the next letter all the way through the end of the alphabet. This is a common technique in Hebrew poetry that, in this case, shows that Lady Wisdom is wise from A to Z. This particular poem seems to be crafted in order to highlight the wise woman as a hero of the highest order.[46] Further, in the Hebrew ordering of Scripture the book of Ruth follows Proverbs. Thus, we can view the hymn as a prelude for the remarkable story of Ruth—a wise woman in her own right.

In Proverbs 9, we met Lady Wisdom as she invited us to her life-giving feast and offered a few words of wise counsel, beginning with the fear of the Lord (9:10). This, of course, was in stark contrast to the rival Lady Folly who at first sounded like Wisdom, but in the end her invitation was a scam and her food was poison.

Now, in Proverbs 31, we are poetically invited to observe a wise woman amid daily life, observing her ways as a wife, mother, and entrepreneur. This poem is a microcosm of the kingdom of God wherein his ways extend into every cultural activity, from home to neighborhood to work and beyond. While the woman's ways apply to the whole wide world, the poem zooms in on the day-to-day, ordinary routine of her life, reminding readers that wisdom is inexhaustibly profound, yet immensely practical.

In this short space, we will quickly highlight ten traits of this valiant and wise woman gathered from the hymn.

1. Wisdom as a Woman

What is the significance of Wisdom being a woman in Proverbs? Is it merely grammatical since the Hebrew word for "wisdom" (*hokmah*) is a feminine noun? Or is it something deeper? This question cannot be answered completely or with absolute certainty. But it merits some reflection, even if briefly.[47] To begin, the fact that Wisdom is a woman yields an opportunity for us to honor women in the whole of creation. While there are important, and often emotionally and culturally charged, discussions concerning the roles of women and men and how they relate to one another in the church, home, and beyond, our purpose here is simply to pause in honor and admiration of women as imagers of God who uniquely contribute to the goodness, truth, and beauty of God's world.

We are reminded of the language from Proverbs 8:22 where "wisdom" (feminine) was "brought forth"[48] at the beginning of God's works, and it is women who are especially designed by God to bring forth imagers of God into his world for the advancement of his ways in all creation. This is hardly the end of the woman's gifts to the world, however. As is readily observed in Proverbs 31, childbearing is but one of many remarkable contributions of women in God's world.

At the risk of overgeneralizing, women attend to and nurture creation—not least other human beings—in special, God-like ways that are often different from men. For their home, they aren't satisfied with four walls and a roof. Instead, women turn a generic space into a beautiful place where family, food, and hospitality happen. The tastes, smells, and laughter that fill a family's kitchen and make lasting memories are most often the result of a woman's wise touch. It is understandable why so many men, when reflecting on their fathers, express appreciation and respect. But upon reflection of their mothers, tears quickly flow.

This is not a reduction of women to childbearing or homemaking. By no means! As the poem of Proverbs 31 illustrates, women are infinitely capable in business, administration, leadership, finance, and more. But lest we rush to scratch the culture's (at least Western culture's) itching ears for equality, let us not ignore the unique and distinctive wonders of women.

On the other hand, we must not forget that for much of history (and in some cultures even today) women were strictly consigned to the home, oppressed by overbearing male headship, and reduced to childbearing and household chores. This is far from the wife and mother we meet in Proverbs 31. This wise woman flourishes *from* her home *into* the rest of society where she contributes to the common good—both of her household and to the broader cultural *oikonomia* (the Greek term for "household" and the source of the word "economy"). She is not limited to the home, but she is liberated by the culture of love and support from her husband and children who praise her and call her blessed (31:28).

2. She Fears the Lord (31:30)

Both the acquisition of wisdom and proper application of wisdom requires starting in the right place—namely, the fear of the Lord. We have given significant attention to this above, so we will limit our comments here. We must not, however, neglect the opportunity to point out again that the fear of the Lord is fundamental to wise living.

The brilliance of the wise woman is that since she begins in the proper place, she aligns with the proper goal (Greek: *telos*) of loving God and neighbor. And because of the right beginning and end, she carries out her activities in the proper way in between. In other words, she walks wisely in every time and place.

3. She Values All of Creation (Material and Immaterial) and Flourishes

For the Western church, there is a tendency toward a dualism that prioritizes spiritual matters over physical ones. This may be seen in Christian devotional practices that stress prayer but give no consideration to physical work or exercise for one's overall health. One might also experience an emphasis on evangelism (the verbal proclamation of the gospel) that is divorced from any consideration of meeting the physical needs of the poor.

For clarity, this is not an either/or. Verbally proclaiming the good news of Jesus is imperative for Christians, and so is the command to clothe the naked, feed the hungry, and care for orphans and widows.

To prioritize the spiritual over the physical is to divide the kingdom of God in a way that is inconsistent with Scripture. This is not to say that duality does not exist. But subjecting one to the other (in either direction) misrepresents God's world and how his grace is at work redeeming the whole of creation.

To return to the point at hand, the wise woman values the whole of creation. She provides food for her household (31:14); she picks out the best wool and flax and works with her hands (v. 13); she values a vineyard (v. 16); "she opens her hand to the poor, and reaches out her hands to the needy" (v. 20); she makes clothing and sells it at the market (v. 24). This is not the way of one who finds little or no value in the material world. This is the way of the wise who understand wholeness and well-being, especially when their talents are directed toward others.

4. She Is Trustworthy (31:11)

The wise woman's uprightness bookends the poem, beginning with verse 11, "The heart of her husband trusts in her," and in verse 29, "Many women have done excellently, but you surpass them all."

All that is accomplished between verses 11 and 29 is laced with justice and equity. In the woman's parenting, farming, teaching, business, and regular household activities her moral character is impeccable, worthy of praise as her children and husband show in verse 28.

This wise woman is trustworthy at every level. When given a task, she is sure to see it through. When left alone, she does not steal or engage in immorality or laziness. At all times and places, public and private, she honors the Lord, and he blesses her.

5. She Speaks with Wisdom (31:26)

We can no doubt think of people who talk a lot, yet never say anything of value. Such word-vomit is nauseating and contributes nothing to the world or to one's well-being, especially when done by an adult. In fact, it steals from the world by taking away God-given time for more useful activities, or even quiet reflection.

This is never a worry around the wise woman. While she is busy with various other responsibilities, she does speak. And when she does, she speaks with wisdom.

What might this mean? As we saw in Proverbs 9, the wise woman speaks with understanding and insight for how we ought to live in God's world. This understanding is not naive or simple. Rather, it recognizes the complexities of life. It acknowledges sin's effects on God's creation and calls out for us to walk in his way, avoiding the broad and seductive path of Folly.

The whole of Proverbs, then, is the wisdom that is found in Lady Wisdom's mouth, ordering our lives in accord with a good, loving Creator. When she speaks, we do well to hear and obey.

6. She Willingly Works with Her Hands (31:13)

That Lady Wisdom is a hard worker should not surprise us here. We noticed this above as we considered Proverbs 9, and the hymn of Proverbs 31 reinforces this admirable quality. This wise woman knows no laziness.

Further, she is entrepreneurial: "She perceives that merchandise is profitable" (v. 31:18). While related to hard work, entrepreneurship is quite another thing. An entrepreneur sees opportunities that others do not. Like artists, entrepreneurs see what could be or what ought to be; and they are able to turn these "coulds" and "oughts" into reality. This is part of the image of God at work in human beings. We are able to see into creation and extract its potential in ways that further the cultural mandate to keep and cultivate the ground (Gen 2:15).

The entrepreneur acts upon and creates many opportunities for herself and others. These opportunities can be misdirected, promoting the way of folly rather than wisdom. But this is not the case with the wise woman.

7. She Takes Responsibility and Serves Her Family (31:13–22)

While it is important to affirm that women are capable of more than mere household chores and motherhood, we must not neglect the great virtue of a woman who not only delights in household responsibilities but excels at them.

As we've just seen, the wise woman is quite the entrepreneur and businesswoman, but not to the neglect of her family. Two important features of the wise woman's character are her leadership and service. Contemporary readers should avoid reading the household duties in verses 13–22 as a job description for women in general or stay-at-home moms in particular. The tasks, themselves, are important and praiseworthy for the good order of a household; and they are best shared among the various members of the home. The wise woman of Proverbs 31 leads in such a way as to ensure that things are taken care of at home. In other words, her management skills are extraordinary.

Her service must not go unnoticed as well. Where do we see this wise wife and mother complaining? Where is the chip on her shoulder about getting her hands dirty with lowly, blue-collar tasks? It is nowhere to be found. She delights in the service of others, exemplifying the virtue of humility so highly praised in Proverbs.

EXAMPLES OF HUMILITY IN PROVERBS

When pride comes, then comes disgrace; but wisdom is with the humble. (11:2)

The fear of the Lord is instruction in wisdom, and humility goes before honor. (15:33)

The reward for humility and fear of the Lord is riches and honor and life. (22:4)

This wise wife and mother delights in serving her family, her neighbors, and the world. As my pastor so often reminds me, "She takes the low place—like Jesus."

8. She Cares for the Poor (31:20)

As neighbor-love insists, this wise woman considers the needs of those around her, even those outside of her socioeconomic sphere. The poor are not to be despised but should be loved and served. Is this a picture of generosity? Most certainly. But it's much more.

To attend to the poor is to forsake oneself. Some, of course, may serve in a soup kitchen or nearby shelter in order to satisfy community service expectations; but not this woman. She considers it a basic responsibility of a Godfearer to care for one's neighbors, especially the least of these. This ought not be done for attention or praise, but out of love, in the spirit of Paul's instruction to the Philippians that we "regard others as better than ourselves" and "look not to [our] own interests, but to the interests of others" (Phil 2:3-4). Especially we must serve those who cannot or will not say thank you in return.

9. She Invests and Earns Profit (31:16, 24)

In verse 13, we observed Lady Wisdom's knack for creativity and entrepreneurship. Now, in verses 16 and 24, we recognize her investment skills.

At least two features are striking here. First, the wise woman loves God, and she does not despise money. Many would hear the previous statement as contradictory: "If I love God, shouldn't I despise money and material things?"

Money is a curious phenomenon of civilization that brings out both the best and worst of the human condition. Christians often recall Paul's warning from 1 Timothy 6:10 that "the love of money is a root of all kinds of evil." For one's love to be rooted in money—that is, in creation itself and what creation can give—is idolatry, which is a great evil. The proper root of love (and fear) is the Creator himself, the King of creation. This is the ever-important vertical dimension that is the highest human allegiance and orientation. But it isn't the only orientation.

This brings us to the second feature. The wise woman does not fear earning profit in business; in fact, she expects it. Economics is a basic reality of human community and civilization. The exchange of goods and services is critical for the survival of cities, towns, and even small communities. The moment that any group of people cooperate together toward one another's well-being, a local economy has emerged.

We will avoid the many aspects of macro- or microeconomics, but we must not be naive about it either. Irrespective of one's view of the best economic system, Christians should advocate for an exchange of goods and services that most corresponds to God-love and neighbor-love for any given time and place. Why? Because wisdom always aligns with the law of God, summarized by Jesus in the Great Commandment (Mark 12:29–31).

At this point in the hymn we observe the wise woman actively participating in the local exchange of goods and services. If verses 16 and 24 were about Lady Folly, this would frighten us, for we would expect her economic character to be greed and exploitation. But when we learn of the wise woman earning a profit, this encourages us, for we can trust that her family and neighborhood will enjoy the benefit of her love and generosity.

This is a timeless truth for any civilization. For some, this should motivate greater activism in earning a profit and wisely stewarding resources. For others, it is a call to consider how others (family, your neighborhood, the broader community) benefit from your profit. Is your motto "more for me" or "flourishing for all"? This is not a case for handouts or entitlements. Rather, it is a call for thoughtfulness and consideration of how God-love and neighbor-love regulate our resources and fiscal activities.

10. She Is Not a Worrier (31:21, 25)

This is a remarkable, and often understated, trait of the Proverbs 31 woman. To fear the Lord properly means that there is nothing more to fear. Psalm 112:7 reminds us that for the righteous whose hearts are firm in the Lord, "they are not afraid of evil tidings" (or bad news).

Does this wise woman not fear because she believes nothing bad will ever happen? Certainly not. Instead, she is wise enough to understand that amid struggle, suffering, pain, and difficult circumstances, God is trustworthy and in control. Thus, her "heart is steady, [she] will not be afraid" (Ps 112:8a).

Wisdom the Human

Proverbs 31 quite rightly serves as a popular text on Mother's Day and other occasions where godly women are recognized. Even in contemporary Jewish tradition, the hymn to the wise woman is often sung each week at the Sabbath table. But might it be appropriate for exhorting men as well?

While this great poem awakens our senses to the beauty of a wise woman, it need not be limited to women. Instead, its application is for everyone—male and female, all who image God.

Wisdom is not partial to men over women or women over men. The book of Proverbs seems well-balanced in this respect, calling the reader time and again to "hear your father's instruction and do not reject your mother's teaching." Further, the two dominant characters in the book are two women (Wisdom and Folly), while the assumed listener and student of wisdom is a son (Hebrew: *ben*).

Wisdom's call is for all who will hear, and her way is for everyone. Men and women alike must walk in her way, beginning with the fear of the Lord and enabled by the Spirit of God.

Raymond Van Leeuwen observes that Proverbs 31 is notably similar to the acrostic poem of Psalm 112.[49] This psalm describes a man who fears the Lord and may be seen as the masculine complement to Proverbs 31.

Considering the inclusive nature of Wisdom's call and the illustrations of wise living seen in Proverbs 31 and Psalm 112, at least two themes deserve brief attention as they concern all people at all times and places.

1. The More We Imitate Lady Wisdom, the More Human We Become

Here, we recall St. Irenaeus's important insight that "the glory of God is a living [human being]."[50] As we have seen, wisdom is life-giving and life-promoting. In this way, it joins the ranks of few other life-giving sources mentioned in Scripture, such as the Father, Son, and Spirit (see especially John 5–6), as well as the Scriptures themselves.

As imagers of God, humans are the crown of creation, endowed with remarkable potential and ability for promoting God's ways in his world. And the degree to which we both live according to God's ways and promote God's ways through our work in his world is the degree to which we live wisely as God intended from the beginning. In other words, the wiser we live, the more human we are, for true wisdom humanizes us. Derek Kidner echoes this point in his discussion of Proverbs 8:22–31, writing that "to turn from [wisdom] is nothing less than to choose one's own unmaking. To find it, at any cost, is nothing less than life."[51]

This is accomplished in any number of ways from farming to pharmaceuticals, rubbish removal to robots, smart cars to skyscrapers, airplanes to accounting—and much more that we could list as human achievement. This is part of the creative capacity of humans. We are not only capable of seeing what is, but we can imagine what *ought* to be, actualizing the potential that God has built into creation for the betterment of life in God's world. This is the continuation of the original Great Commission in Genesis 2:15 to cultivate and keep the garden.

Other ways that wisdom humanizes us include:

1. Wisdom alerts us to the innate value of all creation. All creation is good because it is God's.

2. Wise living does not view the material (or physical) part of creation as good and the immaterial (or spiritual) part as bad, or less good. Proverbs 31 is particularly insightful here as Lady Wisdom is praised for her works—the majority of which concern the material world. Does this discount the spiritual dimension? Certainly not. It requires a person whose spirit is properly ordered to God on the vertical level to wisely engage with the rest of creation at the horizontal level. This follows the "love God, love others" pattern and order.

3. Wise living embraces the human responsibility over all of creation. All time and space belong to God, and his imagers were created to steward his world. As Psalm 115:16 says, "The heavens are the LORD's heavens, but the earth he has given to human beings." Wise living gladly takes responsibility for promoting righteousness, justice, goodness, and love in God's world.

4. Wise living is holistic. Humans are physical and spiritual creatures. Wise living takes this into account by attending to the whole of our humanness. The scholar will do well to cultivate a healthy physical exercise routine in order to get out of their head now and then. Likewise, the bricklayer will want to designate time for regular reading or stimulating conversation to avoid intellectual atrophy. The counselor schedules time to talk with and be encouraged by others

after hours of listening to complicated life circumstances. God calls us to love him with all our heart, soul, mind, and strength. Wisdom compels us to consider our vocations and daily routines so that all our being is active toward love for God.

5. Wise living always corresponds to love for God and neighbor. This axiom for life cannot be left behind in our Lord's Day liturgies. So ingrained is the God-love / neighbor-love shape (a cruciform shape) into reality that it must inform all human decision-making. International diplomacy, architecture, financial services, medicine, education, and beyond all find their "ought" in this double-love imperative.

6. Wise living is missional living. The promotion of God's ways in his world includes telling unbelievers of the Christian's hope in God and the work of his Son, Jesus. And it includes works of love, generosity, justice, and goodness for God's and others' sakes. Wise living is, to recall Matthew 5, salty and bright.

2. The More We Imitate Lady Wisdom, the More Christlike We Become

Jesus was and is the most human person ever to live. How do we know this? As the second Adam, the virgin-born Christ was unstained by sin, despite temptation, and he walked in obedience to God the Father all his days. Christians do not seek to recover the image of the first Adam, but of Christ, the second Adam. He is the power and wisdom of God (1 Cor 1:24), in whom all the fullness of wisdom and knowledge dwells (Col 2:3), and he is the very image of the invisible God (Col 1:15). We model our way after the one who is the Way, Truth, and Life as we pray, "Your kingdom come. Your will be done, on earth as it is in heaven" (Matt 6:10).

SUGGESTED READING

☐ Proverbs 31:10–31

☐ Psalm 112:1–10

☐ Psalm 128:1–6

Reflection

What character traits most stand out to you from the wise woman of Proverbs 31:10–31? Why?

_____

_____

_____

_____

_____

At different points in this chapter we discussed how dualism often finds its way into the Christian worldview and life. Where do you detect this in your life?

_____

_____

_____

_____

_____

The hymn of Proverbs 31:10–31 is applicable for both men and women, as discussed above. Where does your life most align with the example from the wise woman? Where does it least align? Ask God to give you the grace to see and attend to your ways that they may better reflect his ways in the world.

_____

_____

_____

_____

_____

8

WISDOM'S WAY
IN THE WORLD

If you have a money problem, the answer is not money.
The answer is the Lord. ... Our business is always with
God first, and he is the best business partner
in the universe.

—Raymond C. Ortlund Jr., *Proverbs: Wisdom that Works*

Friendship, Finances, and Family

We have focused the bulk of our attention on the themes
found in the first nine chapters of Proverbs, followed by
a chapter dedicated to Proverbs 31. Our approach serves
to frame our reading and experience of Proverbs in light
of the whole of the Bible and in accord with the author's
original intent. Further, it equips us with the necessary
tools to understand the whole of Proverbs and how it
invites all people to heed the way of the Lord and to walk
in the way of the Lord.

Up to now, we have spent little time in the more memorable portion of Proverbs, chapters 10–30. Within these

chapters are found a variety of themes related to ordinary life (including friendship, finances, marriage, leadership, anger, alcohol, and prayer) and many of the pithy, quotable bits of wisdom that are relevant to people in all times, places, and cultures.[52] This chapter will briefly outline and illustrate wisdom's way through the themes of friendship, finances, and family according to Proverbs. These are not exhaustive but merely illustrative and instructive for how the many themes of Proverbs naturally harmonize with the whole of the book when considered in light of the core components of wisdom we have discussed.

SIX KEY POINTS

Proverbs' content is so relevant that the applications to daily life are endless. How does all that we have discussed relate to the rest of the book of Proverbs and to contemporary Christian living? Here are six primary things we have noted.

1. We identified the key contours and ingredients of wisdom.

2. We articulated wisdom's role in the Christian worldview.

3. We explored the meaning of the "fear of the Lord."

4. We considered the relationship between wisdom in Proverbs, the person of Christ, and their relationship to creation.

5. We explored the fundamental role of the two ways represented by Lady Wisdom and Lady Folly in Proverbs 9.

6. We observed the wise woman from Proverbs 31 as the consummate human being and the exemplar of wisdom's way for all people, at all times and places.

Wisdom's Way in Friendship

Proverbs introduces the theme of friendship in Proverbs 7:4–5: "Say to wisdom, 'You are my sister,' and call insight your intimate friend, that they may keep you from the loose woman, from the adulteress with her smooth words." The parallelism is strong here, promoting sincere, intimate, and honest friendship. I often define a friend as someone who loves you enough to make you mad when (not if) you need it.

This is precisely the friendship pictured in 7:4–5. This friend is close enough to detect when another is considering an adulterous decision and loves him enough to confront him about it. Adultery here is not less than physical infidelity to one's spouse, but infidelity to God is also in view. Forsaking the way of wisdom in favor of folly is the epitome of unfaithfulness to God.

This wise friend recognizes the way of wisdom and righteousness and carries as much concern for his friend's walk as he does his own. Any wounds inflicted by this friend are well meant and trustworthy, "but profuse are the kisses of an enemy" (27:6).

Why is this the approach of a wise friend? Because he fears God more than he fears others. A sincere friend is less concerned about what others think of him and is more concerned about the spiritual, physical, mental, and emotional health of his friend. His friendship begins with the fear of the Lord and is oriented toward flourishing relationships founded on love, truth, and justice. These friends are not mere acquaintances but rather "true [friends who] stick closer than one's nearest kin" (18:24).

Selflessness of Friendship (17:9, 17)

A wise friend forgives. Proverbs 17:9 teaches, "One who forgives an affront fosters friendship, but one who dwells on disputes will alienate a friend." Further in 17:17, "A friend loves at all times."

How does forgiveness foster friendship? First, by not thinking too highly of self. Grudges come from offensive comments and actions inflicted against us, and our refusal to forgive the offense breeds bitterness that erodes friendship. While comments and actions may be legitimately hurtful, a wise friend can overlook the offense as he is more concerned with his friend than with himself. Such friendship resonates deeply with Paul's exhortation for Christians to imitate Christ who "emptied himself" (Phil 2:7) on our behalf and was obedient even to the point of death on a cross.

Secondly, friendship fosters forgiveness because it imitates the character of God. If wisdom is first an attribute of the Triune God, it should not surprise us that wise friendship mirrors God's character by willingness—even eagerness—to forgive. Why does God forgive? He forgives out of his loving and merciful nature without compromising justice. Likewise, wise friends are honest about sin and folly and are not surprised by others' hurtful assaults. They understand that forgiveness fosters friendship; thus, they are slow to be offended, preferring instead the love and shalom of a friend.

Self-Giving Friendship

Wisdom's way in friendship is more than selfless, it is self-giving. In other words, wise friendships model Christ.

The book of James (arguably the Proverbs of the New Testament) reminds us, "Thus the scripture was fulfilled that says, 'Abraham believed God, and it was reckoned to him as righteousness,' and he was called the friend of God" (Jas 2:23). Further, Jesus teaches us in John 15 that "no one has greater love than this, to lay down one's life for one's friends" (John 15:13).

Faith plays a foundational role in our relationship to God, making it possible for us to join his family and be welcomed into friendship with him. And Jesus carries the point further that there is no greater friendship than when one friend is willing to die for another.

In other words, by faith we enter into both family and friendship with the one who laid down his life for us. Not only does God make possible a way for us to have friendship with him, but he secures this way for us in the person and work of Jesus, who is the Way—and who modeled true friendship for us through his sacrificial death.

Does our friendship resemble that of Christ? Are we willing to give up even an evening for another, much less our lives? May we strive for self-giving friendship and may Proverbs 18:24 characterize us: "Some friends play at friendship but a true friend sticks closer than one's nearest kin."

Wisdom's Way with Money

Economics is a basic and necessary part of any society. While the term "economics" means more than the exchange of goods and services, it is not less than that. Our economics today revolves around material currency we call money—bills, coins, and the like that represent monetary value.

The Bible has quite a lot to say about money, and Proverbs contributes substantially. Here we observe four major themes drawn from Proverbs regarding one's personal approach to finances. The theme of money is interwoven with other important themes in Proverbs such as work versus laziness, honor versus dishonor, and good versus bad leadership. We will narrow our focus, however, to personal financial matters.

Honest and Just Dealings

Two often-quoted proverbs regarding money are Proverbs 11:1 and 22:7:

> A false balance is an abomination to the LORD,
> but an accurate weight is his delight. (11:1)

> The rich rules over the poor,
> and the borrower is the slave of the lender. (22:7)

The first proverb highlights the important theme of honesty and justice in one's financial dealings, while the other states the danger of debt—especially debt owed to a specific person. On the former, God expects honesty in all matters, as clearly stated in the ninth commandment and reinforced in Proverbs 6:16–19 as one of six things God hates. Dishonesty with one's mouth or one's money is an abomination to the Lord, undermining his way in his world.

Justice in one's dealings corresponds to God's own nature. He deals in righteousness and equity and calls those who fear him to do the same. As Psalm 25:8–9 teaches: "Good and upright is the LORD; therefore he instructs sinners in the way. He leads the humble in what is right, and teaches the humble his way." Further, we recall the words of the prophet Micah: "And what does the LORD require of you but to do justice, and to love kindness, and to walk humbly with your God?" (Mic 6:8).

Generosity

What is more Godlike than giving? The entire drama of the Bible tells of this good and giving God who, despite human sin and rebellion, continued graciously to give to his people, even giving his Son to die in the place of sinners. Now, God gives more by offering the gift of eternal life, available to all who believe in his Son, Jesus, and are restored to fellowship with the Father. And the gift continues as God gives us his Spirit to indwell and empower us as we learn to walk again in his world that he has given to us.

If this is the true story of the world, how could we not be generous?

Generosity takes multiple forms. Time, talents, and treasures (or money) are often cited, and rightly so, but generosity is deeper than these. It requires the constant emptying of oneself in the service of God and others. It affects the giver as much as the receiver, reminding her that "less of me and more of Christ" is the good life. And, Christ is the greatest treasure one could both possess and give.

Deception of Wealth

Wealth gives the impression of security, but is it so? Proverbs 18:11 states, "The wealth of the rich is their strong city; in their imagination it is like a high wall."

A steady income, strong retirement plan, and a healthy investment portfolio are wise assets for a hopeful future; but we must not rest our ultimate hope in them. Job loss, medical bills, economic recession—any one of these is enough to bankrupt the wealthy. When things are going well financially, we imagine that we are untouchable. Yet, when the unexpected strikes, we learn how fragile life is and how our wealth is not such a strong city after all.

Inheritance

"The good leave an inheritance to their children's children, but the sinner's wealth is laid up for the righteous" (Prov 13:22). Wisdom is by nature traditional, and one way to hand it down is through the family inheritance.

Inheritance is generally thought of as a sum of money, land, or various possessions that are bequeathed to children and grandchildren when the parents and grandparents die. Indeed, it is good to order one's estate such that a material inheritance can be passed on to subsequent generations, both for their ability to carry on family culture and place and to assist with financial realities.

But what about families who have no land or money to speak of? What inheritance do they pass on? The inheritance of wisdom is even greater than land or money. This is the greatest asset that one can acquire in life, and it is the most valuable heirloom handed down for generations (8:11).

Buying Wisdom

Recently a friend commented to me, "You can't buy wisdom." I immediately agreed, then later recalled that

Proverbs insists that we do, in fact, buy wisdom and truth: "Buy truth, and do not sell it; buy wisdom, instruction, and understanding" (23:23).

I confess that the meaning of this proverb (and a similar one in 17:16) does not immediately jump out at me. Why would we be encouraged by "buy truth, wisdom, and understanding"?

The answer lies not in the literal exchange of money for wisdom. Instead, the exchange takes place in the human soul when we give up our attachment to the temporary in exchange for the eternal.

To "buy wisdom" is to invest one's hope and love in that which is eternal, namely, the participation in life, love, goodness, justice, righteousness, and anything else that bespeaks the nature and activity of our loving God. This division between temporal and eternal should not be understood as a division between physical and spiritual, or material and immaterial. As we have already seen, the whole of creation is good because it's God's; even the material world remains an important part of God's redemptive plan as evidenced in the incarnation—God who became flesh.

Instead, exchanging the temporal for the eternal plants one's faith, hope, and love in God, allowing these three to animate our lives as we walk the way of wisdom in God's world.

Wisdom's Way in Family

To consider family is to consider relationships, a topic about which Proverbs has much to say. It is also to consider God's design for people to rule over his world in community, beginning with the family in relationship with God. Thus, we will heed Proverbs' instruction about relationships in general with special attention to the family.

In chapter 2 we learned from Derek Kidner that while the family is not everything in Proverbs, "the home remains the place from which this teaching emanates, and whatever threatens its integrity is viewed here with profound concern."[53]

Husband-Wife Relationship

Honor Over Annoyance

Proverbs offers rather memorable comments about the "nagging" or "contentious" wife, such as these two verses:

> It is better to live in a corner of the housetop
>> than in a house shared with a contentious
>> wife. (21:9)

> It is better to live in a desert land
>> than with a contentious and fretful
>> wife. (21:19)

The same could certainly be said for the nagging or contentious husband as well. The important thing to note here is less about gender and more about the relationship—that we should be mindful of how we speak to one another and how it affects the culture of the home. This overlaps with Proverbs' many verses on talking and listening, but Proverbs 21:9 and 21:19 underscore how our often thoughtless words create tension and annoyance over time. In Proverbs 27:15 these mindless comments are likened to a "continual dripping on a rainy day." They are less sinister than gossip or slander, but equally as damaging in the long run.

The preferred alternative is for husbands and wives to honor one another in all their ways, both privately and publicly. The husband's desire should be to praise his wife like the husband of the valiant woman in Proverbs 31:28b–29. This isn't empty flattery in front of others, but sincere admiration. For this is the way of love, especially neighbor-love toward one's spouse.

Integrity Over Impurity

Integrity in general is a prominent theme in Proverbs (14:2, 15:33, 18:12), and especially in the family, integrity is expected to fill the home and characterize the relationships therein. Proverbs 20:7 says, "The righteous walk in integrity—happy are the children who follow them!" The English Standard Version renders the second half of this verse, "blessed are his children after him!"

Indeed, the righteous do walk in integrity. This shouldn't surprise us as walking is a major metaphor in Proverbs and the rest of the Bible, and acting with integrity corresponds to God's character, the life of Christ, the order of creation, and particularity of circumstance. It can be handed down through generations such that "his children are blessed after him."

Sexual integrity toward one's spouse is especially important, as the imagery is vivid and warnings are strong in Proverbs. In accord with the strong warnings about the seductive woman from Proverbs 7 (see chapter 6), we do well to heed the pleas of the narrator, who insists that we listen and not allow our hearts to turn aside to her ways—ways that lead to death (7:25-27).

For many, we should hear this as a straightforward warning to be ever on guard against the seductiveness of sin, especially sexual sin. For others, the seductive woman of Proverbs 7 may represent materialism, consumerism, selfishness, greed, sloth, or some other expression of the wicked way.

Integrity in the husband-wife relationship fertilizes the soil of the home to produce a flourishing family. Integrity removes the fear of "what if" between spouses and children. It reinforces confidence in relational fidelity between husband and wife, and thereby reflects the relational fidelity of God to his people. And even if (God forbid) infidelity does occur, the story of our God is one of relentless faithfulness to his people, his bride. May God grant us perseverance toward such faithfulness.

Parent-Child Relationship

Listening

Much of Proverbs is a narration of a father to a son (or child) regarding wisdom, which instructs us in the importance of listening in the home. Proverbs 13:1 teaches, "A wise child loves discipline, but a scoffer does not listen to rebuke." The family emphasis on listening leans heavily toward kids listening to parents and grandparents, and this is critical. Yet, more generally, wisdom teaches us to be good listeners regardless if we are the child or the parent.

In other words, children, listen to your parents and receive their wise instruction; parents, listen to your children also, not necessarily to receive wise instruction but to understand them better, to honor their existence by lending an ear and not just a tongue, and so that your instruction to them can be well suited to their situation— for wisdom isn't one-size-fits-all. It is particular.

Discipline

I often remind my kids, "Rules exist because maturity doesn't." Much could be said about this, but the point is that the reason we have rules in our house is for the good of our children until they mature. Some rules (or laws) are established by the state or nation in which we live. But others are installed by mom and dad, such as, "Hold my hand in the parking lot." Why? Because my kids are currently still quite young, and I'm only just beginning to trust the older two to be wise with how safely they behave in a parking lot.

Now, if this rule still exists when my kids are twenty years old and above, something is seriously wrong. This is an example of people serving the rule instead of the rule serving people, and this stifles maturity. Rules properly installed and defined should promote maturity and should be lifted once maturity manifests.

What has this to do with discipline? When just rules are broken for unjust reasons, punishment is necessary for the good of the rule breaker and for the sake of love and peace in the home. Such discipline must be commensurate with the crime and carried out in a loving fashion. But neglecting discipline would be wrong for it fails to spur on the child, indeed the entire family, toward love for God and others.

Legacy of Wisdom

Part of the beautiful nature of family is legacy. We pass down tradition, heritage, and culture from one generation to the next, seeing it altered and modified along the way. Legacy travels with these changes and reflects the ways and values of multiple generations.

Proverbs expects that wisdom will be laced through the legacy of generations (recall Prov 20:7 from above). It is cultivated and acquired throughout life and is understood when it begins properly with the fear of the Lord. Then, like a family recipe, it is handed down for future generations in families who carry on the tradition of walking in the way of the Lord. This is the mood and motive in Deuteronomy 6:1–4:

> Now this is the commandment—the statutes and the ordinances—that the LORD your God charged me to teach you to observe in the land that you are about to cross into and occupy, so that you and your children and your children's children may fear the LORD your God all the days of your life, and keep all his decrees and his commandments that I am commanding you, so that your days may be long. Hear therefore, O Israel, and observe them diligently, so that it may go well with you, and so that you may multiply greatly in a land flowing with milk and honey, as the LORD, the God of your ancestors, has promised you.

Proverbs expands on this idea, illustrating what a life of fearing God and keeping his commandments looks like in the home and beyond.

These brief reflections on friendship, money, and family are only the beginning of wisdom's way in Proverbs. I pray they provide clarity and coherence for how the contours and components of wisdom discussed throughout this study are the core ingredients of wise living in God's world. Proverbs' many themes are saturated with these wisdom ingredients, ever motivating Godfearers to love him and love others.

May we walk in his way, and may "the grace of the Lord Jesus Christ, the love of God, and the communion of the Holy Spirit be with all of you" (2 Cor 13:13).

SUGGESTED READING

☐ Key verses on wisdom and friends:
   Proverbs 7:4–5; 12:26; 14:20; 16:28; 17:9, 17; 18:24; 19:4, 6–7; 22:11, 24; 27:6, 10

☐ Key verses on wisdom and money:
   Proverbs 8:11, 18–21; 11:1, 4, 15, 24–26; 15:27; 16:8; 17:16; 18:11; 19:17; 21:6; 22:7, 9, 16; 23:4, 23; 27:23–24; 28:27; 30:7–9

☐ Key verses on wisdom and family:
   Proverbs 10:1; 13:1–2; 15:20; 17:2, 6, 17, 21; 19:13, 18, 26; 20:7, 20; 22:6; 23:13–14, 22–25; 27:8; 28:7, 24; 29:3, 15, 17; 30:11, 17, 21–23

☐ Psalm 119

Reflection

Choose one of the topics discussed in this chapter (friendship, finances, or family) and consider how the core wisdom ingredients outlined in chapter 2 instruct us in wisdom's way.

_____

_____

_____

What is another topic from Proverbs not discussed in this chapter (such as leadership, laziness, education, etc.) that deserves attention in your life? How would you connect the essential wisdom ingredients to help you better understand wisdom's way in that area?

_____

_____

_____

What are three significant takeaways from this book?

_____

_____

_____

CONCLUSION

As we close our study, I pray your journey into Proverbs is only just beginning. Its relevance and application to everyday life is endless, even beyond the simple how-to's and best practices in parenting, finance, politics, work life, friendship, and so on. Proverbs' roots are sunk deep into the overarching story of the Bible, reminding us that this is still our Father's world, and we play an important role.

Thus, we end our study of Proverbs as we began, by admitting that we must learn to walk again. We therefore exhort Godfearers everywhere to "Get wisdom!"—which begins with the fear of the Lord. God's wisdom is not limited to the church, the home, the checkbook, or to elderly people. Lady Wisdom calls out into the streets to all who will hear, issuing an invitation to come in and dine with her. May we hear and obey this call, for her feast offers life eternal.

Such also is the call of the Lord Christ. And this is no coincidence, for Jesus is the power and wisdom of God who invites us to dine with him where life is abundant and eternal. Through Jesus' life we see God's wisdom and way reestablished in his world and advanced by his people. Let us therefore join the faithful people of God, who walk in the way of Christ and declare his kingdom come on earth as it is in heaven.

APPENDIX: TIPS FOR READING AND TEACHING PROVERBS

So if it seems to you that you have understood the divine scriptures, or any part of them, in such a way that by this understanding you do not build up this twin love of God and neighbor, then you have not yet understood them.

—St. Augustine of Hippo, *On Christian Doctrine*

When it comes to teaching Proverbs, unity is paramount. For all of its popularity, breaking Proverbs apart into small pieces and spreading it out in a proverb a day type devotionals is not helpful for grasping the book's coherence, its significance in the story of Scripture, or its theological depth as it anticipates the life and ministry of Jesus. Here are some tips for teaching Proverbs.

Tip 1: Connect the Wisdom of Proverbs to the God of the Bible

Proverbs makes no apology for Yahweh, the God of Abraham, Isaac, and Jacob as the Creator and the beginning of wisdom. Rather, it assumes this as truth and explains life lived *coram Deo*, before the face of this God.

Everything is his (all time and space), meaning all of our life should be directed by this beginning—indeed, by this God.

To replace "the beginning of wisdom" with any other god or thing is to undermine the central agenda of Proverbs. This is much like the creation narratives of Genesis 1–2, where the Scriptures make no apology and offer no further explanation about this Creator God. Instead, Genesis uses the creation story as a counternarrative to other creation stories (myths) in the ancient Near East. This one stands above the rest as the true story of the world.

Proverbs, too, offers a counternarrative of its own. This counternarrative builds upon Genesis' creation narrative but is even more concerned with the way people live in God's world. And this is not limited to the descendants of Abraham. Lady Wisdom calls out to all people as her teaching transcends Jew and gentile distinctions and her scope is as wide as creation. Thus, we must connect Proverbs to the God of the patriarchs, Moses, David, and the prophets to authorize Wisdom's call in the Creator, ground it in the creation, then mobilize Godfearers and followers with humble confidence before God and in the world.

Tip 2: Connect the Wisdom of Proverbs to Jesus

The apostle Paul makes clear that Jesus is the "power and wisdom of God" (1 Cor 1:24) in whom dwells "all the treasures of wisdom and knowledge" (Col 2:3). We do well, then, to connect Proverbs' wisdom with Jesus, though we must be careful of jumping to Jesus too quickly and squelching the sage insight of Proverbs.

When teaching Proverbs, we must remember and recognize Jesus all along the way.[54] We remember Jesus as the one who is Wisdom incarnate, and we remember Jesus as the one who walked in wisdom perfectly, manifesting wisdom's way *in* the world and modeling wisdom's way *to* the world. Jesus is thus the hero of Proverbs, the perfect Son who "heard ... [his] Father's instruction, and [did] not reject [his] mother's teaching" (Prov 1:8).

Tip 3: Connect the Wisdom of Proverbs to the Great Commandment and the Great Commission

Christians rightly recognize the Great Commission (Matt 28:16–20) and the Great Commandment (restated by Jesus in Matt 22:37–40; Mark 12:29–31; and Luke 10:25–28) as high points in the Bible for understanding Christian living and mission. In other words, these are "the Greats" of the Bible. We must link our interpretation and application of Proverbs with the Greats of Scripture, underscoring the unity of Scripture from beginning to end.

Here I echo St. Augustine, who suggested that any interpretation of Scripture that does not build up love for God and neighbor has misunderstood the text. When we walk wisely in God's world, full of faith, hope, and love, sharing the good news of Christ with the world in word and deed, we simultaneously promote both the Greats and God's way of wisdom. It is truly impossible to do any one of these without also doing the others.

Tip 4: Connect the Topics of Proverbs to Wisdom Ingredients

Proverbs 1–9 provide the interpretive key to the rest of the book.[55] These chapters serve as a prologue of sorts, answering the "Why?", "How?", and "How do you know?" questions of the proverbial disciple, or child of wisdom. Most of the book (chapters 10–31) offers dozens of the short, memorable sayings for which Proverbs is best known. Chapters 1–9 ground these otherwise random nuggets of wisdom in God and his creation, connecting them with true wisdom from above (Jas 3) and not mere tips for successful living.

As we consider specific topics from Proverbs, then, we do well to note the various wisdom ingredients that most resonate with the topic and link our interpretation and application to true wisdom manifested in the world. See chapter 8 of this study for examples.

Tip 5: Preach Proverbs 31 on Mother's Day *and* Father's Day

I have enjoyed the privilege of teaching Proverbs 31 on both Mother's Day and Father's Day. Yes, Father's Day! Some might think this inappropriate or ill-fitting for Father's Day, as Proverbs 31 teaches us about the amazing and valiant wise woman. In no way should we downplay the fact that the valiant woman is, in fact, a woman. Yet we should recognize that she represents more than women. She represents the whole of humanity.

The wisdom exhibited by the valiant woman of Proverbs 31 is the wisdom to which Proverbs beckons us all. Women and men ought to be known for our fear of the Lord, hard work, thoughtfulness and service to our families, care for the poor and marginalized, prudent investment and financial management, and much more.

Tip 6: Make It Matter!

We must not miss the fact that Proverbs prizes the ordinary. Friendship, work, money management, talking, eating, marriage, parenting, discipline, politics, and other everyday matters of life are found in the middle—not in the margins—of Proverbs. The theology of Proverbs is thick and integral to its overall aim, but equally so is the ordinariness of Proverbs' subject matter. It reminds people from every social class, race, gender, and country that their day-to-day life matters to God, and their day-to-day life is an opportunity (even a responsibility) to promote wisdom's way in God's world.

In our explanation and application of Proverbs, let us be diligent to emphasize its unity and coherence, connecting the dots between the theological and practical and showing how wisdom truly impacts all of life in every time and place.

RECOMMENDED READING

Craig G. Bartholomew and Ryan P. O'Dowd. *Old Testament Wisdom Literature: A Theological Introduction*. Downers Grove, IL: InterVarsity Press Academic, 2011.

> For a helpful introduction to wisdom literature generally, and the doctrine of wisdom specifically throughout the Bible, Bartholomew and O'Dowd's volume is excellent and accessible. Additionally, Bartholomew's smaller volume, *Reading Proverbs with Integrity*, Grove Biblical Series (Cambridge: Grove Books, 2001), is particularly helpful as an introductory guide for reading and teaching Proverbs.

Michael V. Fox. *Proverbs 1–9*, The Anchor Yale Bible Commentaries. New York: Doubleday, 2000.

> Fox offers piercing insights into Proverbs from a contemporary Jewish perspective. He offers careful analysis and great concern for wisdom's continuity with Torah law, connection with creation, and ancient Near Eastern background that helpfully illuminates the text.

Derek Kidner. *The Wisdom of Proverbs, Job and Ecclesiastes: An Introduction to the Wisdom Literature.* Downers Grove, IL: InterVarsity Press, 1985.

> Kidner's work has become classic for the study and teaching of Proverbs. His knack for cutting to the heart of the matter practically with a keen eye to theological significance is exemplary. I heartily recommend this introductory work by Kidner as well as his other commentary work on Proverbs and Psalms.

Tremper Longman III. *How to Read Proverbs, How to Read Series.* Downers Grove, IL: InterVarsity Press, 2002.

> Longman's work is among the best of contemporary, cutting-edge research on Proverbs and wisdom literature. He is a sure guide through the text for technical, theological, and practical matters. Longman's commentary, *Proverbs*, Baker Commentary on the Old Testament Wisdom and Psalms (Grand Rapids: Baker Academic, 2006), and his *The Fear of the Lord Is Wisdom: A Theological Introduction to Wisdom in Israel* (Grand Rapids: Baker Academic, 2017) are also highly recommended. Finally, he provides good insight in "Book of Proverbs 1" in *Dictionary of the Old Testament: Wisdom, Poetry and Writings*, ed., Tremper Longman III and Peter Enns (Downers Grove, IL: InterVarsity Press, 2008).

Raymond C. Van Leeuwe. *Proverbs*. The New Interpreter's Bible, vol. 5. Nashville: Abingdon, 1997.

> Van Leeuwen has become, for me, a favorite commentator on Proverbs. His depth of insight into Old Testament matters (grammatical, theological, and otherwise), mixed with care for canonical connections and insights, are always stimulating. Further, his attention to wisdom as a Christian worldview yields much fruit for whole-life application of the text. His various articles on Proverbs and wisdom are also valuable for study and teaching; for instance, "Liminality and Worldview in Proverbs 1–9" in *Semeia* 50 (1990), and two articles, "Book of Proverbs" and "Wisdom Literature," in *Dictionary of Theological Interpretation of the Bible*, ed. Kevin J. Vanhoozer [Grand Rapids: Baker Academic, 2005]).

Bruce K. Waltke. *The Book of Proverbs: Chapters 1–15*. New International Commentary on the Old Testament. Grand Rapids: Eerdmans, 2004.

> Waltke's work on Proverbs has spanned multiple decades now and remains valuable for study and teaching of the text. His work balances the technical with the practical, with an eye toward the theological. It will doubtless stand the test of time and will bless God's people for generations to come.

NOTES

1. For a survey of biblical interpretation, see Alan J. Hauser and Duane F. Watson, eds., A History of Biblical Interpretation series, 3 vols. (Grand Rapids: Eerdmans); Gerald Bray, *Biblical Interpretation: Past and Present* (Downers Grove, IL: InterVarsity Press, 1996); Craig G. Bartholomew, *Introducing Biblical Hermeneutics: A Comprehensive Framework for Hearing God in Scripture* (Grand Rapids: Baker Academic), 113–250. For historical views on wisdom literature, including Proverbs, see Craig G. Bartholomew and Ryan P. O'Dowd, *Old Testament Wisdom Literature: A Theological Introduction* (Downers Grove, IL: InterVarsity Press Academic, 2011); Al Wolters, *The Song of the Valiant Woman: Studies on the Interpretation of Proverbs 31:10–31* (London: Paternoster, 2001). Moreover, Will Kynes's work regarding the genre of wisdom literature is helpful and not lost on me; one example is Will Kynes, *An Obituary for "Wisdom Literature": The Birth, Death, and Intertextual Reintegration of a Biblical Corpus* (Oxford: Oxford University Press, 2019). My point here is less about the genre of wisdom literature and more about the uniqueness of the book of Proverbs.

2. See Bruce K. Waltke, *The Book of Proverbs: Chapters 1–15*, New International Commentary on the Old Testament (Grand Rapids: Eerdmans, 2004), 50–55.

3. See Al Wolters, *The Song of the Valiant Woman*, 15–29.

4. Raymond C. Van Leeuwen, *Proverbs*, The New Interpreter's Bible (Nashville: Abingdon, 1997), 5:21. Also Waltke, *The Book of Proverbs: Chapters 1–15*, 36–37.

5. See Tremper Longman III, *Proverbs*, Baker Commentary on the Old Testament Wisdom and Psalms (Grand Rapids: Baker Academic, 2006), 23–26.

6. This is not to suggest that the wisdom of Proverbs is somehow inauthentic. As many in the Christian tradition (including Augustine and C. S. Lewis, for example) have argued, "All truth is God's truth." Therefore, we should expect to agree with other cultures (even other religions,

at times) about certain things. But we must always connect truth and understanding back to the one true Creator, Yahweh. For more on ancient Near Eastern wisdom traditions see Richard J. Clifford, "Introduction to Wisdom Literature" in *Proverbs*, The New Interpreter's Bible (Nashville: Abingdon, 1997), 5:1–16; Roland E. Murphy, *The Tree of Life: An Exploration of Biblical Wisdom Literature* (Grand Rapids: Eerdmans, 1997), 151–75.

7. Adapted from Longman, *Proverbs*, 24–25, and Bartholomew and O'Dowd, *Old Testament Wisdom Literature*, 74–76.

8. Raymond C. Van Leeuwen, "Wisdom Literature," in *Dictionary of Theological Interpretation of the Bible*, ed. Kevin J. Vanhoozer (Grand Rapids: Baker Academic, 2005), 848.

9. These components of wisdom are modified from Bartholomew and O'Dowd, *Old Testament Wisdom Literature*. Bartholomew and O'Dowd cite Raymond Van Leeuwen as the originator of these "categories." Also, special thanks to Dr. Ferris "Chip" McDaniel for his suggestions in refining the language of the ingredients.

10. Derek Kidner, *The Wisdom of Proverbs, Job and Ecclesiastes: An Introduction to the Wisdom Literature* (Downers Grove, IL: InterVarsity Press, 1985), 20.

11. Al Wolters, *Creation Regained: Biblical Basics for a Reformational Worldview*, 2nd ed. (Grand Rapids: Eerdmans, 2005), 2.

12. Wolters, *Creation Regained*, 5.

13. Van Leeuwen, "Wisdom Literature," 848.

14. Van Leeuwen, "Wisdom Literature," 848.

15. Raymond C. Van Leeuwen, "Liminality and Worldview in Proverbs 1–9" in *Semeia* 50 (1990): 113.

16. Plantinga and Rozeboom, *Discerning the Spirits*, xi. Also from Wolters, *Creation Regained*, quoting Old Testament scholar James Fleming: "For the wise man of the book of Proverbs ... 'wisdom ... was wrought into the constitution of the universe,' so that 'man's wisdom was to know this divine Wisdom—plan, order—and attune his ways to it.' Consequently, 'wisdom meant conforming to the divine constitution. One must find out what it is, then order himself accordingly.' In a word, 'wisdom is ethical conformity to God's creation'" (29).

17. William D. Reyburn and Euan McG Fry, *A Handbook on Proverbs* (New York: United Bible Societies, 2000).

18. Further discussed in chapter 4.

19. See Van Leeuwen, "Liminality and Worldview in Proverbs 1–9."

20. Emphasis mine.

21. C. S. Lewis, "Is Theology Poetry?" in *They Asked for a Paper: Papers and Addresses* (London: Geoffrey Bless, 1962), 165.

22. Longman, *Proverbs*, 102.

23. Eugene H. Peterson, *Christ Plays in Ten Thousand Places: A Conversation in Spiritual Theology* (Grand Rapids: Eerdmans, 2008), 41.

24. Henri Blocher, "The Fear of the Lord as the 'Principle' of Wisdom," *Tyndale Bulletin 28* (1977): 27.

25. Rowan Williams, "The Intellectual Renewal of the Church," Vision Lectures, May 11, 2016, Wycliffe Hall, Oxford, UK, https://www.youtube.com/watch?v=MHa9etSOL7Y.

26. Irenaeus of Lyons, *Against the Heresies 4.20.7* in The Ante-Nicene Fathers, vol. 1, ed. Alexander Roberts and James Donaldson (Peabody, MA: Hendrickson, 2012), 490.

27. "The Nicene Creed," in *Documents of the Christian Church*, 4th ed., Henry Bettenson and Chris Maunder, eds. (Oxford: Oxford University Press, 2011), 27.

28. See "Date and Authorship" in chapter 1.

29. Daniel J. Treier, *Proverbs and Ecclesiastes*, Brazos Theological Commentary on the Bible (Grand Rapids: Brazos, 2011), 48.

30. Treier, *Proverbs and Ecclesiastes*, 48.

31. Treier, *Proverbs and Ecclesiastes*, 50–51.

32. Treier, *Proverbs and Ecclesiastes*, 51.

33. Treier, *Proverbs and Ecclesiastes*, 51.

34. Treier, *Proverbs and Ecclesiastes*, 57. Proverbs 8:22–31 is a theologically tricky passage with a turbulent history. While Treier arguably gives too little attention to translating *qanah* as "created," he offers a sound approach, saying neither too little nor too much on a passage that is ambiguous at best for Christian readers.

In agreement with Van Leeuwen, we also suggest that the Wisdom of Proverbs 8 has multiple references, similar to the prophecy of Isaiah 7:14. Proverbs 8 is not prophetic in the same way as the Isaiah passage. Instead, just as Isaiah 7:14 seems to refer both to Ahaz's day and to the birth of Jesus, so too Proverbs 8 is multi-referential (see Van Leeuwen, *Proverbs*, 96–99). This we see as a function of theological unity across the canon of Scripture.

35. Special thanks to Dr. Ferris L. "Chip" McDaniel for this helpful articulation.

36. Waltke, *The Book of Proverbs*, 435. In part of this section, Waltke is quoting from William McKane, *Proverbs: A New Approach* (Philadelphia: Westminster, 1970), 360.

37. Van Leeuwen, "Wisdom Literature," 848.

38. Waltke, *The Book of Proverbs*, 436, emphasis added. See also Proverbs 8:4–11, noticing the address to all people.

39. Irenaeus, *Against the Heresies* 4.20.7, 490. This is a more common rendering of the quote by Irenaeus. A more literal translation reads "for the glory of God is a living man" or "human being."

40. See Alexander Schmemann, *For the Life of the World: Sacraments and Orthodoxy* (Crestwood, NY: St. Vladimir's Seminary Press, 1973).

41. "Knowledge" in Proverbs 1:7 is the Hebrew word *da'ath*, while "wisdom" in 9:10 is the common word for "wisdom" in the Hebrew Old Testament, *hokmah*.

42. Michael V. Fox, *Proverbs 1–9*, The Anchor Yale Bible Commentaries (New York: Doubleday, 2000), 301–302.

43. The King James Version of Galatians 5:22 reads: "But the fruit of the Spirit is love, joy, peace, longsuffering, gentleness, goodness, faith."

44. Bartholomew and O'Dowd, *Old Testament Wisdom Literature*, 110.

45. Wolters, *The Song of the Valiant Woman*, 28.

46. Wolters, *The Song of the Valiant Woman*, 3–14.

47. For a scholarly survey of interpretation and exegesis on the feminine nature and persona of wisdom, see Waltke, *The Book of Proverbs*, 83–88.

48. This is borrowed from the NIV translation of this verse. See chapter 5 for more on the interpretive and theological history surrounding this passage.

49. Van Leeuwen, *Proverbs*, 5:260.

50. Irenaeus, *Against the Heresies* 4.20.7, 490.

51. Kidner, *The Wisdom of Proverbs*, 24.

52. For a helpful list of themes with associated verses and sub-themes found in Proverbs, see Longman, *Proverbs*, 549–78.

53. Kidner, *The Wisdom of Proverbs*, 20.

54. See chapter 5 of this book for further discussion.

55. See Craig G. Bartholomew, *Reading Proverbs with Integrity*, Grove Biblical Series (Cambridge: Grove Books, 2001).

LEXHAM PRES